31/5/22

Daisy Turnbull

50 Questions

A guide to fostering communication and confidence in young adults

TO ASK YOUR

Teens

Hardie Grant

BOOKS

Daisy Turnbull is a teacher and director of wellbeing. She has taught at St Catherine's School in Sydney for eight years, and before that taught across school systems, including at a behavioural school working with students with varying challenges. Before going into teaching, she worked in interactive advertising as a producer and in strategy roles. Daisy is an accredited Lifeline crisis support counsellor and regularly volunteers on the crisis support line. She is the mother of two children, and holds a Combined Bachelors degree in Arts/Commerce, a Graduate Diploma of Secondary Teaching, and a Master of Arts in Theological Studies. She is also an obsessive crocheter.

TO LUCY AND MALCOLM, WHO SURVIVED
MY TEENAGE YEARS. THANK YOU, I LOVE YOU.

AND THANK YOU TO THE TEENAGERS WHO HAVE TAUGHT
ME FAR MORE THAN ANY CURRICULUM COULD.

Contents

Because your question searches for deep meaning, I shall explain in simple words.

— DANTE ALIGHIERI

Foreword

It's so important for parents to engage with teenagers by asking questions rather than just making rules and issuing directions. This book starts with that key perspective. It asks those serious questions that are on young people's minds, about things like sex, consent, feelings, peer and intimate relationships, and wider responsibilities. As a parent, aunt, uncle or close friend, you don't need to know the answers – just be willing to join the conversation!

As adolescent thinking moves from the simply transactional to more complex personal and societal considerations, engagement with genuinely inquisitive adults can provide one of the richest environments for promoting development. Adolescent brains thrive on challenges, activities, language and novelty.

Contrary to much popular thinking, teenagers greatly enjoy talking through tough issues with those who have genuine experience. Leaving 15-year-olds to answer the challenges put by other 15-year-olds often doesn't lead to much progress. By contrast, spirited interactions with warm and engaged adults is often the best way forward.

This book doesn't back off from the hard questions. It provides a no-nonsense guide. It addresses the issues that every teenager needs to face at some time. With the assistance of those who really care, that journey can be so much easier. It can also be fun, for both teenagers and their parents. We all need to take the time to grow together. I hope that this book will stimulate many others to take that time.

PROFESSOR IAN HICKIE
AM MD FRANZCP FASSA FAHM FRSN
CO-DIRECTOR, HEALTH AND POLICY,
BRAIN AND MIND CENTRE, THE UNIVERSITY OF SYDNEY

ASSOCIATE PROFESSOR ELIZABETH SCOTT
DMEDSC FRANZCP
PRINCIPAL RESEARCH FELLOW, BRAIN AND MIND
CENTRE, AND CONSULTANT PSYCHIATRIST

Introduction

Having been a secondary teacher for over 10 years, I have been asked some wonderful, and incredibly difficult, questions by teenagers and their parents. Teenagers are, by definition, a work in progress. There is something fascinating about their constant back and forth, the pulling away and coming back to the nest, the testing of boundaries, the desire for independence while also demanding psychological safety. One of the key things I have learned in teaching teenagers is that experiences are hugely important to them. Experiences literally shape their brains, their characters, their hearts and their relationships.

Often the students with behaviour issues have parents who step in way too much – or not at all, sometimes to the point of neglect. In general, teenagers whose parents give them more responsibility are more responsible. Teenagers with a lot of co-curricular commitments might do them because their parents want them to, but they'll only excel in them when they are intrinsically motivated. Parents who focus on strengths have better relationships with their kids. It is important to note here that this book is written for teenagers who are neurotypical, although I do include some information about neurodivergent teens. Where my first book, *50 Risks to Take With Your Kids*, was written for the overparenter (which is most of us), this is written for the parents of your average teenager – who is not really average at all.

Without getting too deep into the technicalities, you become a 'teenager' at 13 years of age, and an adult at 20. But for the purposes of this book, I'm going to think of teenagers as actually starting at 11 or 12, given that a lot of students starting high school are only 12.

50 Risks mentions my kids Jack and Alice quite a bit, because when I wrote it they were three and six and I drew on my lived experience as a mother. This book does not include much of Jack and Alice, because they are not yet teenagers (unless I go seriously over deadline), but it reflects my lived experience as a high-school teacher. (Note: student experiences featured within these pages are anonymised.)

Where *50 Risks to Take With Your Kids* focused on the practical, underpinned by psychological evidence, *50 Questions to Ask Your Teens* goes beyond the practical. For all my jokes about making teenagers sit on hold to a utilities company for hours on end (and they should definitely do that at some point), there are far greater complexities to teenage life, and to parenting a teenager, than that.

What do you want your relationship with your kids to be like when they are grown up? And how do you intend to get there?

I volunteer at Lifeline, a 24-hour telephone crisis support service in Australia. Many of the calls I take there distress me, but the ones that I really need a self-care break after are from women in their 60s and 70s who are lonely because their kids never visit or call them. I want to say, 'Call your kids and tell them you've been calling Lifeline. That will make them realise how crap they are being.' But of course I can't do that, and in many cases there are reasons for distance.

But how do those parents get to that point, and how do you (and I) not?

The teen years are crucial to this.

This book is being written in what I pray to God is the tail end of a pandemic in Australia. There are two concepts that have bubbled along throughout the COVID-19 pandemic. The first is the impact 'toxic stress' has on children and teenagers, even once life goes back to 'normal', whatever that looks like. The second is the importance of relationships and connection.

Many relationships were strained during the pandemic, which is why these two topics are so interconnected. The external stress of the pandemic, lockdown, working and studying from home, and all that screen time (and associated screentime guilt) affected everyone, but especially teenagers.

The risks of social isolation are real; the loneliness of social isolation can lead to mental-health issues, such as depression. Research has shown that much of this social anxiety has stemmed from not having access to the opportunities for empathy and socialisation that teenagers need in order to properly individuate from their parents.

But toxic stress and external impacts on family life are not new. Wars, famines and nuclear disasters have impacted generations of children long before ours. Those experiences, just like this one, have all shown that what's important is how family relationships shape and protect children's development through these storms.

I write with hope for the future. I write with hope that the teenagers today, the ones I teach, especially, will make the world better, and safer, and far, far kinder than it is now. We don't know what the mid- to long-term impacts of this pandemic will be on teenagers, but I hope that it has taught us all the importance of protecting our mental health through relationships, connection and conversation.

Why questions?

My first book focused on risks, but for this one I've taken a different approach. That's because teenagers are a very different beast to young kids. Their inner worlds can be very hard to access. When you think about talking to teenagers, their responses generally involve grunts or one-word answers. How was school? Fine. What's up? Nothing. The questions in this book are designed to start conversations, to give you some data or perspective on your teen's life, and to foster an ongoing connection with them. Some questions deal with topics you may not have considered covering with your teen, and you can, of course, ask the questions you're comfortable asking, in a way that suits you. Not every question will be one you feel comfortable asking, and maybe there is someone else who could.

The questions in this book are designed to be approached in the spirit of naive inquiry. Naive inquiry is a style of questioning used when you may have no information, or only one piece of information. You might say, 'I noticed x, what's that about?', as though you have no idea what x is, you've never seen an x, you don't even know how the x got there. There is no judgement in naive inquiry. There is also no 'yes' or 'no' answer to a naive inquiry.

'I saw something about polar bears the other day. What do you reckon about polar bears?' You are in fact nurturing your inner Seinfeld – 'What is the deal with [insert topic here]' – approaching the everyday with curiosity and openness.

If the x we are talking about is, say, a murder weapon covered in blood, sure, your level of questioning might get more pointed as it goes on, but conversations with teenagers need to be started openly and honestly. As soon as a teenager feels you judging them, they will shut down. This book isn't about eliminating all judgement, but it *is* about eliminating judgement when you ask a question.

When I was training to be a counsellor at Lifeline, we were taught to not ask 'why', because it carries a level of judgement. 'Why did you do that?' has judgement attached, because even by asking the question you're implying the reason isn't obvious, and often this question is asked after the fact, when nothing can change. No teen (or human) wants advice on something that is in the past. Similarly, if something is done and dusted, what's the point in asking why?

How was that for you? What did you think of this? When do you feel like this? Who is someone you talk to about this? Can you walk me through your thinking? These are all better questions.

Why conversations are needed

Teenagers are famous for disconnecting from their parents. In psychology this is actually called individuating and, much like bankruptcy, it happens very slowly and then all at once, as Ernest Hemingway wrote. Conceptually, it is something that you want to happen – that is, you want your teenagers to become adults – but in practice, as parents, we often try to stop it happening in small ways.

During the teenage years, you want to set up points of connection that allow for a deep and authentic relationship that will remain even when your kids are adults. This does not mean there are 50 conversation threads that you need to keep going with your teen, like some supercharged WhatsApp group. Instead, the questions act as door-openers to conversations and experiences that connect your child back to you.

I am a knitter. I'm not great at it, but I do it quite a bit. One style of knitting is called fair isle. The knitter will hold up to dozens of colours of yarn in one hand, picking up different colours to create a pattern on one side of the piece and a bit of a mess on the other. As a parent of a teenager, the strands of yarn that you hold will be used less as their jumper is made, and instead your teen will rely on their own strands. But if those connections are strong, they can seamlessly be added in, with flecks of yarn from their teenage years filling in a new solid colour of their adult selves.

When we talk about connecting with teenagers, it's really about the when, why, where and what. But also, just because I'm a history teacher and I like to round the W questions out, there'll also be a who chucked in there. Sometimes, the who is not you. This is important to note.

WHY

Why you are connecting with your teen is absolutely the most important thing to consider. For the most part, these questions are designed to take you out of a place of authority and instead open a thread of communication that allows you to regularly return whatever your teen chooses to serve at you. There are also conversations that you need to have with your teenagers, because they are topics your teenager needs to know about. Too often, as a teacher, I have encountered the assumption that 'someone else is talking about it' – particularly around the topic of consent and sexual assault. You cannot expect others – teachers or friends – to have these conversations for you and still control the message. If you let everyone else talk to your teen about sensitive subjects, but fail to do so yourself, then you have no one else to blame for them learning the wrong stuff, or stuff that is in conflict with your own values. Sometimes these conversations are incredibly awkward, but that is not a reason not to have them.

I think there is a disconnect between schools and parents, where each often expects the other to have taught teenagers pretty basic and important stuff. This assumption has been bad at best and catastrophic at worst. (I'm thinking specifically here about the expectation that someone else has taught your teen about sex and consent – oh wait, no, it's fine, PORN DID IT for us – more on that in Differences, starting on page 196.)

This book is for parents, and in my experience as a parent, and as an educator of over a decade, and as someone who has marketed products to teenagers, *and* as someone who was in fact once a teenager (and is still the height of most teenagers) – the buck stops with you. You, the parent, have to have these conversations with your teenagers and teach them these skills. If they say, 'Yeah, yeah, I know about this, we talked about it at school', then make sure they tell you what they know. If they can't explain something to you – or, in the case of practical skills, demonstrate it – then tell them to pull up a chair, roll up their sleeves or put the kettle on.

WHEN

When you connect with your teen is also super important. If there is a bowl of Weet-Bix in the vicinity, you are almost certainly going to be in a rush. If they are stressed about exams or an upcoming test, it is definitely not the time. Pick your moment wisely. A good 'when' can be while driving, or in other moments of transition. Can you walk together instead of driving sometimes? Rituals also make for great whens, like the Saturday morning supermarket shop, or breakfast at a local cafe. The when can be during jobs, such as while unpacking the dishwasher together, or folding laundry.

The great thing about structuring chats around a job or ritual is that this creates a clear time limit. Not all of these questions will lead to hour-long conversations; no one wants to spend three hours talking to their teen about porn. So creating natural start and end points to these conversations can be helpful too. In her book *The Bonsai Child*, psychologist Dr Judith Locke suggests this technique when listening to a rant: say 'Sure, you can rant about Susie while I make dinner, but then you have to help me do x.' Make sure these conversations are constructive and don't descend into endless rants.

WHERE

Depending on where your teen is at developmentally, the where can vary. Some teenagers protect their room (even if it is shared) so fiercely you might assume they are harbouring a known fugitive rather than some really dirty socks. In that case, don't walk into their territory and demand to talk about respect and feelings, because that is not going to go down well – you've undermined your point before you've even started. But even if your teen is happy for you to talk to them in their room, or even to talk to you in your room, aim to connect in spaces that are more neutral while also being private. What I'm saying is, do not talk to your teen about coercive control with a younger sibling doing their homework right beside you.

WHO

Well, it's you, right? Or maybe not. One of the first ways to slowly let go of your teen is to accept that there may be other adults, and peers, who they want to have these conversations with. These people will not form a secret police who feed intel back to you, no matter how helpful that would be. Some of the questions in this book might make you want to put the book down and say, 'I'm NEVER having that conversation with my teen!' Okay, then who will? Does your teen have other adults, or trusted peers, who they can have these conversations with? If not, are there people you can encourage them to form these relationships with?

Evidence tells us that teenage girls need 'aunties' who they can talk to about their problems. Dr Steve Biddulph refers to them as 'feisty older women'. The same is true for young men. Harvard psychologist Professor William Pollack talks about the benefits of young men having 'an extra dose of Dad' to develop healthy relationships and manage the expectations placed on young men. And, if Dad is not available, good male role models can have especially beneficial effects. We also know that the first people teens talk to about their problems are their peers. I go into the importance of peers in section 3 (starting on page 128).

They say it takes a village to raise a child. That village will come in handy with your teen as well, especially if you are a single parent or if you and your partner have values that your teen is in opposition to. If you feel uncomfortable having some of these conversations, then okay, don't have them – but make sure someone else is.

WHAT

Well the what, dear reader, refers to the questions on the following pages – all 50 of them. A lot of these questions should be relatively easy to broach, but others might be a bit more confronting. When confronted with a topic that could be difficult to talk about, ask yourself these questions: What will be difficult about it? Why might it be important to talk about? How can you best raise it?

Teenagers

To be a teenager means a lot more than it did a few generations ago, both in society and psychologically. Prior to World War II, teenagers either studied (if their families could afford it) or they worked. In 1880 in New South Wales, for example, children aged seven to 14 had to attend school for at least 70 days every six months, which meant children attended when they weren't needed for farming. In 1916 the requirement was for two hours in the morning and two hours in the afternoon every school day, which as a working mother actually makes me break out into hives. In 1940 school attendance was required from ages six to 15.

So until World War II a lot of teenagers across Australia were working. It was really after the war that the 'teenager' became a thing in Western societies. In the postwar era, teenagers got to spend the whole day at school with other teenagers, and so had a chance to develop their own customs. Teenagers have always looked to those around them to work out how to do the whole 'life' thing (see question 23, page 182). After World War II, 'those around them' were no longer family, but other teenagers. The teenagery-ness exploded. Being at school instead of at work also meant they had time in the afternoons. They'd be in gangs, walking the streets with other teenagers, acting in mysterious teenager ways, talking about teenager things. After WWII they were heavily influenced by rock 'n' roll, and began to develop their own distinct culture. For example, gangs formed around Sydney between 'bodgies' and 'widgies' – rejecting mainstream values and embracing subcultures around things like that well-known evil, 'surfing', and hanging out in those crack dens of days gone past, 'milk bars'.

And thus the teenager was really born. Life was far easier for them than it had been for the previous generation. Postwar prosperity and a baby boom meant they didn't have to work as much, families lived in bigger houses, they had TVs ... And then the postwar shag-fest was introduced to contraception and parents had fewer children, meaning their kids got more attention, there were fewer mouths to feed, and teenagers often didn't even need to work. This of course led to more time with other teenagers, and more teenager vibes. It was a total mood. And there weren't even memes yet.

The adolescent brain is a strange and wonderful thing. We tend to think a lot about the impact of what teens are and aren't doing – risky behaviour, not wanting to talk or hang out with their parents, and the dreaded 'peer pressure' – instead of what is actually going on inside their noggins. (For more about teenagers' underdeveloped prefrontal cortex, see section 6, starting on page 266.)

Dr Dan Siegel, MD and founder of the Mindsight Institute, has conducted extensive research on the adolescent brain. His book *Brainstorm* is basically my bible on this stuff.

One of the areas he talks about is the need for secure attachment. We know babies need a secure attachment with their parents or caregivers to survive. But actually, we still need secure attachments long after we're able to make ourselves a snack or communicate.

The thing is though, as children become teenagers, they start individuating from their parents (even the ones with whom they have the most secure of attachments) and move towards their peers. This is healthy, it is ancient – it is actually how you survive. If you were a cave teenager and you didn't hang out with other cave teenagers and your cave parents were stomped on by a mammoth, you would be alone, and you would probably die.

Parents should die before their kids, so teens need to have relationships beyond their parents.

This is when the why and who kick in. The why is important, and you probably already know it – kids need relationships because healthy relationships (I'm talking platonic here; we'll get to the other kind later) are the single biggest factor in a person's health, happiness and longevity.

So when your teen is saying 'I NEED to go to that party', to bond with their important who, they're actually not exaggerating – it's kind of an evolutionary requirement. That doesn't mean you have to let them go, but it does mean you should talk to them about their psychological needs, if they don't understand them.

Becoming a teenager who wants to individuate from their parents is normal and natural, but it doesn't mean they get to disrespect you. Actually, it's a bit of a dance that has been going on since teenagers started hanging out together on the porches of their caves.

Step 1: Teenager says to parent 'I want to go to the party'
Step 2: Parent says 'no'
Step 3: Teen starts to rebel
Step 4: Parent gets stricter
Repeat steps 3 + 4 for a few years until the parent has no authority.

It's a bit like a rubber band: the further you pull it, the stronger the snap back.

It is important to remember what your teen needs. In *50 Risks* I introduced Erik Erikson's first four stages of life – trust versus mistrust (up to 18 months old), autonomy versus shame and doubt (18 months to three years old), initiative versus guilt (three to five years), and industry versus inferiority (ages six to 12). Each stage builds on the last. You cannot have a strong stage four if your stage three was not really achieved.

Stage five is identity versus confusion. It lasts the whole period of this book – up to age 18. During this stage, teenagers are learning who they are, and by that I mean who they are as distinct from you. You need to let them become themselves, while also parenting them, loving them and being there for them.

In the first few years as a parent, you are like a shadow ensuring your kid doesn't fall over or break anything. Then you become a bit of a logistics coordinator and coach. In the teenage years, your authority continues to decrease and your omniscience declines. You should become more of a lighthouse – always there and consistent, excellent in emergencies, but not following them around.

This is because at the next stage – 18 to 40 years old – people look to develop intimacy and strong relationships. You need a strong sense of self to do this. Without a strong sense of self, it is hard to have strong relationships, and this won't become apparent until beyond the teen years.

The next stage is the one you as a parent are probably in. Age 40–65 is about generativity versus stagnation. You are working and parenting and contributing to the community. Hot tip: you can't do it all at once, and will focus on one or the other for periods. I am very rarely a good mum and a good employee on the same day. During this period, you are always needed, and your worth feels at its highest. However, if you don't feel needed, your motivation can be low and you may begin to feel worthless, which is a precursor to some mental health issues including depression. It is important to be generative in this period. However you find your value, find it.

Once you hit 65, you reach a period Erikson referred to as 'integrity versus despair'. If you look back on your life and are proud of what you've achieved, be it self, family, career or community, you will feel a strength of integrity. If you don't, you may despair. This is when relationships with family are so important. Relationships are the scaffold of integrity. They make us happy.

The biggest factor in life satisfaction is relationships, according to the Harvard Study of Adult Development, an 80-year-old longitudinal study currently run by psychiatrist Robert Waldinger that looks at what makes someone healthy and happy. If you have strong relationships, you are happier, and you have a good(er) life. More than money, more than career success, relationships matter. Especially your relationship with your kids.

As your kids go between stages five and six and you go through stages seven and eight, allow them to develop their own identity, and their own value, secure in the knowledge that this will help you both have good relationships.

The 'job' of a parent never really ends, it just changes. It can change beautifully and symbiotically, or you and your child can grow apart, leaving you both lonely. Remember, this book is designed to start conversations with your teen that will last you both through all stages of life.

'Adulting is hard.'

– THE INTERNET

Life skills

Never before has a generation of adults complained so much about 'adulting'. 'Adulting is hard' has become a catchphrase, and memes abound about how great early bedtimes are and why regular bill payments suck. I don't blame young adults for hating being adults, especially when, for some, their teenage years were so fun – living at home, free wi-fi, friends just around the corner, laundry washed and folded, dinner cooked ... honestly, it sounds like the best holiday ever. One reason for this disillusionment with adult life, though, is that in their younger years kids often aren't given the opportunity to do things for themselves, and in the teenage years many practical life skills are no longer explicitly taught.

When we are growing up, there are things we implicitly learn, like walking on the correct side of the footpath, or the colour of postboxes. These things are not taught to us, we just pick them up along the way. And then there are things we are taught explicitly, like our times tables or how to dress ourselves.

We need to explicitly teach teenagers how to be adults, just as when they were kids we explicitly taught them to put rubbish in the bin, or to look people in the eye when they said hello. This is by no means an exhaustive list of life skills your teen might need, but it's a starting point. You will be able to modify or add to this list based on your own household's needs, or your own life skills. The goal here is to ensure that your teen will be able to manage life's difficulties, and also make a good housemate and cohabitant – not just for their future, but also for you, right now. These questions are designed to give your teenager some autonomy in the responsibilities they want to develop and design.

/. What can you help with?

Together with any other adults you share the parenting responsibilities with, spend some time thinking about what your teen can do. Not in relation to sports and maths, but in relation to being an adult and a good housemate.

So, firstly start with a list of all the stuff that has to be done at home. These are things like laundry and dinner, but also the other stuff, like school sports admin, managing assignment due dates and all that fun stuff. Write it down.

Next, cross out what your teen is already doing. Then consider the things that aren't crossed out. What can be added easily and slowly to the crossed-out list? Don't start with taxes; that will set them on the path to a life of tax avoidance faster than you can say 'pay me in cash'. Start small. If they're taking out the rubbish, are they

sorting recyclables? If they're doing laundry, are they ironing too? Also, try not to genderise tasks. If you are setting your sons up to take out the garbage and your daughters to unpack the dishwasher, you are unintentionally buying into gender norms that will carry through your teen's life. Try to be aware of them now.

Some of these tasks might fall into what is known as 'the mental load'. This has existed for many, many centuries. (Stone Age meme: 'I am always moving the mammoth bones after dinner and Mr Ugh never appreciates it, he just assumes mammoth bones go out to the midden on their own.') The mental load is everything that happens before you do a task or chore – all the organising and preparation needed before you can 'just do it'. As Eve Rodsky describes in her book *Fair Play*, it's the conception and the planning of something, as well as the execution. And it's finishing the job properly (unlike Mr Ugh).

The mental load encompasses all the thinking and knowing and ordering of online groceries. It is knowing how much milk is in the fridge, which friends have birthday parties coming up and where that bloody orange shirt is for Harmony Day. It's knowing what needs to get done when, delegating if necessary, and making sure it gets done. The mental load is huge, and in heterosexual partnerships and families, it's usually shouldered by women.

Both as a mother and as a single mother, I carry an enormous mental load. I can no longer blame anyone else for the fact I always have to take out the rubbish; it's my job. In fact, a very wonderful and wise friend said about single parenthood, 'There is a strength and vulnerability to it. It is all on you, which is scary, but it is all on you, and you just have to do it, and you can.' And I can.

As your kids become teenagers, they should start to share that mental load. Make sure you are giving your teen tasks that include the whole nine yards – the conception and planning as well as the execution. Or give them the conception and planning while you handle the execution. For example, they can plan and pack for school camp, but you'll make sure they get there on time. Aside from teaching your teen to be a good housemate, increased challenge and competency also brings psychological benefits, and helps to develop their autonomy.

If you have read *50 Risks*, you'll know I go a bit fangirly for Richard Ryan and Edward Deci, who created self-determination theory. This theory condenses a lot of research into an easy to understand model that illustrates what makes us self-motivated and responsible.

The first key element of self-determination theory is autonomy – the trust and responsibility parents give their children. This basically means they're doing stuff on their own.

The second is competency. This relates to the actual ability to do a task. Professor Angela Duckworth writes a lot about the need for teenagers to gain competency in order to develop grit. It is effectively a symbiotic relationship.

A lot of psychological research has been done on giving teenagers small challenges to increase their competency. When every task is that bit more difficult, you feel a sense of achievement for completing it. You can easily adapt this to apply to household tasks, increasing the difficulty and responsibility for your teen over time.

The third part of the self-determination model is relatedness. I cannot put this more plainly: relationships are at the heart of everything. When you feel there is a connection to the people you are working with, or doing a task with, you perform better. We know students perform better with teachers with whom they have a strong relationship.

But there is another reason, beyond chores, to think about what your teenager can do. A strengths-based approach to parenting will make for a better parenting experience in general, and greater communication with your teen. Professor Lea Waters, author of *The Strength Switch*, argues that the strengths your teen may have in one arena (for example, organising their social life) can be channelled into an arena where their strengths may be hiding (such as organising their time to study). Discussing and understanding what your teen's strengths are puts you in a far better position to help them develop skills than reminding them of what they can't do.

It is totally okay to roll one's eyes at doing chores. I roll my eyes at doing my taxes. But make them do it. Bin night, setting the table, cleaning up. Everyone in the family contributes, including the teens. And where in *50 Risks* it was about getting kids doing these jobs so they learn how to do them, for the teens it is so that they can eventually do it all themselves, because the goal is to become a fully functioning adult.

2. What's for dinner?

The ability to cook is a pretty basic requirement of being an adult. A love of food is nice to foster, too. Teenagers should learn to cook out of necessity, but also because it develops an understanding of being a part of a family, a household and, eventually, their own future family.

Preparing meals goes well beyond the actual turning on of the stove or oven, too. This goes back to the topic of the mental load. Sometimes when I ask my kids to do something like set the table, they will wonder what I have done to contribute. Unbeknownst to them, buying the food, cooking the food and cleaning up afterwards is not actually done by house elves.

There are heaps of ways to get your teen into cooking. You could prepare a meal they like together so they can learn how to make it. Some teens might even suggest this so they can one day make it themselves. But not all will.

The internet is awash with recipes, especially 'viral' recipes. Get your teen into the excitement of cooking by tapping into their desire for an Insta-worthy meal. Shows like *MasterChef* might also pique your teen's interest in learning to cook.

Cooking is easy to share, and learning to cook with your teen can be an opportunity for better conversations. There are also psychological benefits to sharing meals, and the preparation of them, to keep families close (as I talk more about in question 48, page 324).

Every culture and every family is different, but a good starting point might be asking your kid which meals from your repertoire they'd like to learn how to cook. For my children the list would probably include bolognese, a roast, slow-cooked things, casseroles, soups, barbecues and salads. (Why yes, I am a white Australian, why do you ask?)

And remember, this is equally important for sons and daughters. The ability to cook is not gendered; everyone needs to be able to do it.

3. How are you going to keep the wolf from the door?

Getting a job as a teenager is not mandatory, nor is it necessarily expected. For the most part, working as a teenager is about earning some spending money. It takes the onus off the parents to provide that money, as well as being good for the teenager's self-esteem – because the best way to improve self-esteem is to know you can do something. Kids with more responsibilities become more responsible, and work, even in the most mundane of jobs, encourages autonomy and develops life experience.

My first job was washing hair at a hair salon when I was 14½ years old. I was so excited to get a job. I worked there every Sunday until I was in Year 11, and each week I would earn around $40. I saved absolutely none of it, but I learned that I liked having responsibility, and that you have to turn up for work. I have known students who are far more responsible

in their part-time jobs than they are in their studies. There is a goodness to that, because then you know they do have that skill, even if it may be misdirected.

Your teen's school might teach the students how to write a CV and a cover letter, or they might not. Either way, there's no reason for parents not to do it as well. This won't require a lot of research, because almost every adult has had a job. Talk to your teen about jobs you got when you were their age, and jobs you didn't get. Help them with their applications and run practice interviews. Ask them typical interview questions, like 'What is a difficult situation you've experienced and how did you overcome it?' or 'When have you shown leadership?' You might know the answers better than they do. Practising these questions with your teen not only helps prepare them for job-seeking, it can also boost their confidence

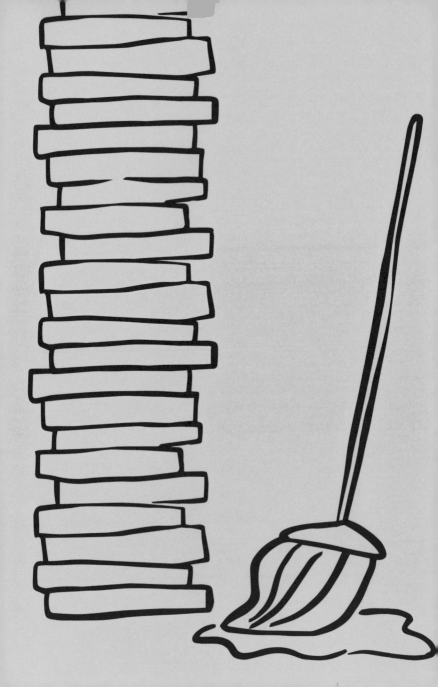

by helping them identify the strengths and experience they already have under their belt.

Talk to them about the minimum wage, about superannuation, about what their rights are at work. I knew a student who thought if she ever said 'no' to a shift she would automatically lose her job, because nobody had told her otherwise. Do not assume your teen knows this stuff.

Also, talk to them about managing their expectations of work. All work is, well, work, even if it's fun sometimes. Their boss might suck, and that's okay – they are learning how to deal with difficult people. Maybe they find the work really boring – well, there's the inspiration they need to study harder so they can get a more interesting job when they finish school. And also, let's be frank, there are boring parts of every job (*cough* school reports). They hate it? Okay, then they've learned what they don't want to do when they grow up. Or maybe they love it, and it gives them some more purpose, and a greater appreciation of all the juggling parents do on a daily basis.

4. What do you do to rest?

Self-care. Face masks (the relaxing kind, not the hygienic kind). Bubble baths. Books.

Doctors will tell you that rest is essential for mental and physical health. But in our increasingly busy lives, rest is not prioritised. Busyness has become a marker of status and success, and while 'self-care' is a new buzzword, getting your nails done isn't going to cut it. We should all be resting every day (and this includes you).

In her book *Sacred Rest*, Dr Saundra Dalton-Smith talks about the seven types of rest people need. They do not all involve sleep, although seven types of nap does sound ideal to me.

The first type is physical rest: sleeping or napping when your body needs to. It may have been a while since you told your teen to have a nap, and they may

have fought the concept of naps when they were younger, but sometimes we do need physical rest.

The second is mental breaks – these are really important for teenagers (and adults), especially when they are studying. Encourage them to break up study routines by going for a walk, staring at the wall (which will rest their eyes as well as their brain), playing a game or listening to music. Your brain needs 5–10 minutes to repair at least every two hours. The same goes for long car drives – rest every two hours.

The third kind of rest is sensory – away from screens, sounds, lights, pings and the dopamine hit of our phones reminding us we are loved and connected. These breaks do not need to be long or righteous (a seven-day digital detox is my idea of hell), but they do need to be intentional. Deciding to read a book or draw rather than look at a screen is an important break that our brains need.

The fourth kind is creative rest. My girlfriend Shentel, who is a designer and creator, has a great approach to this. When she feels blocked creatively she goes for a walk and takes photos of everything she sees. The awe and wonder then inspire her. We all need moments of awe.

Emotional rest is the fifth kind of rest, and one of the most important. Emotional rest means taking a break from pleasing people. This doesn't mean being rude to people, but actually stopping to think about what you want to do, how you feel, and what you need. That doesn't mean you'll actually get it, of course, but knowing it is the first step.

Social rest is the one students needed most during lockdown – time with the people who nourish us. You know you've had a social rest when you feel better after seeing someone. If you don't feel nourished and happier after catching up with friends, then they've probably contributed to your fatigue rather than to your rest. Check in with yourself about what you need.

Finally – spiritual rest. We need to rest our souls. For some that will involve prayer, for others mindfulness and meditation. Some people might choose yoga, walks or being in nature. Shinrin Yoku is the Japanese term for bathing in nature. Even something as simple as looking at a tree for five minutes is known to have physical health benefits.

As a parent, you'll probably read this and think, 'Yeah, I know rest is important.' But how did you know, and how will your teen find out? Talk to them about it. Tell them how you rest, and ask them how they get the different types of rest they need.

And then there's burnout. This occurs when you've been stressed for so long that you're past the point of no return – total mental, emotional and physical exhaustion. You run on empty. Burnout used to be the niche of overworked lawyers or doctors, and mothers juggling work and parenting. Now, it's recognised to be much more widespread.

Burnout occurs when we do not give our bodies and brains enough rest to balance whatever it is that is burning us out (and often up). During the COVID-19 pandemic, many people experienced burnout in different ways and at different times. For teenagers, excessive screen time was a major contributor. I taught during the initial 2020 lockdown and found that the students could not focus for the whole lesson, such was the psychological intensity of an online class. Five-minute breaks between lessons helped, but what students really needed was time with their friends – the one thing we could not give them.

Finally, if your teen is living a life that leads to burnout, they should consider what exactly is burning them out, and how they can restructure their time and their lives. Dr Lisa Damour has written about the importance of a restorative practice. Just like having a rest day from the gym, we need to have rest built into our lives. And sometimes that rest can come in the form of boredom, or soft fascination in something. To need rest does not mean your life is too busy or frantic. Rest should be built-in.

5. What do you know about money?

Just because your teen is able to read and do maths, don't assume that means they understand how money works. Teenagers need to be taught financial literacy. This is true regardless of their family's financial circumstances.

And it's especially the case for women, who are more than twice as likely as men to experience financial abuse. Almost one in five women experience some sort of financial abuse in their lives. And even in great relationships, women's financial independence is often interrupted through parenting and time out of the workforce, costing them not only their current income but also their future earning potential and superannuation for retirement.

So, here are some questions to ask your teen about money:

- What money do you have saved?
- What do you know about tax?
- What do you understand about superannuation or retirement savings?
- What banking fees are you paying?
- What are your financial goals?

I have taught students whose superannuation accounts have been in overdraft because they were paying monthly fees on a $100 balance they accrued at a summer job when they were 15. They need to be aware of how these things work.

There are numerous conversations to have about money and financial literacy with your teen. The first is about cost: mention the cost of things like food, utilities and holidays – not to guilt-trip them, but so they develop a sense of how much things actually cost relative to income.

Explain that work is for a person's purpose as well as to pay the bills. Life costs money. Some parents avoid talking to their kids about money, either because it's a stress in their own lives or because they worry their kids will gloat or be indiscreet. For better or worse, money is a huge part of our lives. Why shield kids from it, when we can instead foster a healthy relationship with it that emphasises the value of hard work? Research shows that most kids in middle-class families in Australia are the richest they will ever be BEFORE they finish school. Why? Because they don't put in the work. That is to say, they will never out-earn their parents or have a better lifestyle than them.

Talk to your kids about budgets and savings, credit cards and debt, to help them understand what goes into providing all the things in their life that they might otherwise assume just 'exist' or grow on trees.

Furthermore, back to that topic of genderising chores, consider how you role-model financial management in your family. Regardless of how you divide up the work of managing money in your family, make sure your teen is being raised to understand that money is everyone's responsibility.

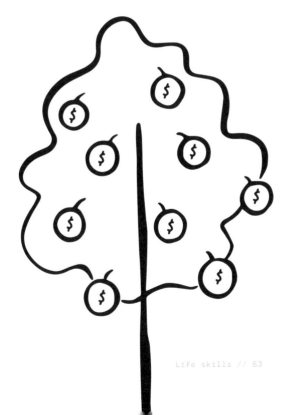

6. How big do you want your world to be?

I want to start by talking about my grandmother Jo. She is 94 and lives down the road from me.

Her world is very small, but once it was huge. Jo went on ocean liners and travelled the world. She was a divorcee before it was normal. She lived in Paddington in Sydney when it was full of artists and beatniks, and has spent over four decades watching it gentrify. When I was young my brother and I would walk with her to Centennial Park and she would know everyone who passed us. Everyone.

But as she aged, her world became smaller. Partly due to mobility, partly due to fear. Her world is very small now. Her front porch on a sunny afternoon. Her front room in the morning when the light shines in. Her sofa and her bed. The TV and opera hour on ABC

Classic FM. That is her world now, punctuated by visits from outsiders: her children and my cousins, the kids and I, her wonderful best friend Linda, the few friends she has who are still alive.

The point is, your world gets smaller as you get older, but the starting point is already smaller than it once was. The global pandemic of 2020 and beyond has shrunk our worlds further still. In one way, teenagers today have infinitely sized worlds, with social media and YouTube channels and group chats. But they are not the whole world. They are not real. Teenagers need a physical world, too.

Their physical world is built from curiosity and adventure, as well as friendships. But these days opportunities for socialising in person after school –

the bus stop, the train station, the park – have been replaced by the internet. Even hanging out at the mall as a social activity has been replaced by screengrabbing online purchases. And that, while huge, is also solitary. We need to promote the idea of teenagers getting out of the house and doing things that build their worlds in ways that are safe and enjoyable. We know that today's teenagers are doing a lot less of the types of activities their predecessors enjoyed. In fact, research tells me that when I was a teenager, I had an extra 100 minutes every day when I wasn't on a screen. What did I do with that time? What are teenagers NOT doing with that time? And what impact is it having?

Encourage your teen to join a sporting team or a music group, or to take up lifesaving, or just let them come home from school slowly, rather than rushing home to tutoring or chores.

If your teen is someone who already experiences their whole world in their rooms and on their screens, try to expand it – go for walks, or reintroduce the kind of family day trips you may have taken when they were young. There is huge psychological benefit in being able to experience awe. This doesn't have to involve huge family hikes – it could be something as simple as a sunset, a sunrise or a storm. There is not much that is awesome, in the literal sense, in their rooms.

Travel is a part of this too. It could be travelling to an unfamiliar suburb, or travelling to a different country. When the pandemic ends, where would you like to travel to? Travel, especially for teenagers, connects you to the world beyond yourself. It makes you realise that there are other places with other people who have lives that are completely different from yours.

I try to build my world out because I know that one day it will be small again. That ability to go to the next suburb or to another country, or to walk the whole day because I am enjoying an audiobook, will go, and I want that downsizing to take time, and to start from a big place. Help your teenager make their world as big as it can be, to share with you and to have on their own as well.

'Character – the willingness to accept responsibility for one's own life – is the source from which self-respect springs.'

– JOAN DIDION

Character

At a certain point in childhood development, we stop talking about kids having 'a great character' and talk about 'character' in and of itself. Character is about what makes a person different, what is innate to them and in them.

The concept of character gets discussed a lot in the light of positive psychology, but it is also ancient and enduring. Prior to Christianity, Stoic philosopher Seneca wrote that people should 'Cherish some man of high character, and keep him ever before your eyes, living as if he were watching you, and ordering all your actions as if he beheld them.' This idea of doing good when no one is watching is universal, and is linked to the idea of treating others the way you want to be treated. Character is not just about doing good (regardless of who is watching), but about how we respond to challenges, how we treat others, and the attitudes we bring to certain situations. Aspects of modern life are causing us to lose touch with this concept.

Are we educating our kids in the concept of character effectively? Are we teaching them to identify character and develop their own inner selves? Do our teenagers do the right thing, the good thing, when no one is looking?

We develop character in different ways throughout our lives. Many of our childhood experiences help us develop character. But some character-building experiences are taught, or experienced, implicitly. And they are taught by you, as a parent. They are what you do when you model behaviour, like saying please and thank you, treating everyone with respect, and not swearing when someone cuts you off in the supermarket car park (rest assured, my children have seen bad driving behaviour role modelled plenty of times).

Much is written about the need for teenagers to be firm and strong in their character, but I think it is also important that there is vulnerability and softness at play. Bravery often lies in vulnerability, not in toughness, and embraces the need for humans to be relational. Our character is built in our integrity, in people trusting us, and in our ability to trust others. A lot of our character and confidence is built before the teenage years, through secure attachment and healthy relationships with parents and carers during early childhood. Don't be fooled into thinking that a strong character is an emotionless one.

To enable our teenagers to develop a strong character, we need to give them opportunities to form, and test, themselves, while feeling secure in the knowledge that they are loved.

I often hear adults talk about things that happened to them when they were kids – moving schools, being bullied, or their parents divorcing. These events can very easily become part of someone's identity – resilience-building in some but an excuse for bad behaviour in others.

I think this is where a person's character really lies – in how they see these events. You very rarely see someone who has achieved great success – be it career, academic or family – who hasn't faced some difficulty.

Even if your kid has gone through difficulties of many kinds, they might be fine, or they might not be. But be careful not to buy into determinism as parents. Our past shapes us, but it doesn't define us. And your teen's future past is happening now, so get shaping!

The stage may have already been set, but the acts are unknown. I must say, when my son turned seven, I thought of the quote variously attributed to Aristotle and St Ignatius Loyola: 'Give me the boy at seven and I'll show you the man.' Yes, there are characteristics and personality traits that will stick with him forever, but how he is going to turn out is still unknown.

The point is, your character shapes you more than you think. Where renowned psychoanalyst Sigmund Freud's aetiology focuses on trauma that defines you (generally involving your mother), proponents of character-based psychology like Professor Angela Duckworth argue that we can grow and shape our character through values and grit.

Alfred Adler, a psychologist writing at the same time as Freud, said 'The important thing is not what one is born with, but what use one makes of that equipment.' Character is not set – that's why children are always given 'character-building experiences'. A lot of these experiences don't really build character so much as they build resilience, which in turn develops character.

This character and past-trauma stuff also leads into the issue of chips. Specifically, the kind that reside on one's shoulder. Almost no one is born to a perfect life. It is very easy to build a mantra based on the idea that 'they had this growing up, I didn't' *chip chip*, or 'they didn't have anything bad happen to them' *chip chip*.

There are two issues here. The first is that the bearer of the chips is partaking in determinism. We all know that's bad now, right?

But the second issue is that maybe the chipper, as it were, doesn't realise that everyone has had difficulties but some are fewer and more hidden than others. I will talk about gratitude in more detail later, but gratitude is one way to navigate out of that chipping cycle.

So remember, as a parent, there are many steps ahead of you, and nothing is set in stone.

7. What are your strengths?

I am not one to talk about the gifts of parenting, because I am very honest about parenting being a constant struggle, with some really fun bits thrown in. But if there was one 'gift' of parenting, it would be that you see the worst of your kids – that is their gift to you. They love you and feel safest with you. And that really is a gift, even if it also means you have to deal with the biggest tantrums from ages two to 52. You are also uniquely placed to see their strengths, and to identify what those strengths are and how your teen can use them.

A friend told me about her six-year-old once having a moment of self-awareness (not what

six-year-olds are known for), and saying on a Friday afternoon, 'I've been good at school all week. I can't be good anymore, I just want to be me.'

What does this have to do with strengths and teenagers? A lot. As a parent you will see the worst of your teen, but that doesn't mean you get to see the worst IN your teen. As parents we love our teens, but that doesn't mean we always like them. This is where strengths can be really helpful, both for you and for them. Professor Lea Waters has researched and written about the benefits of strength-based parenting, where you lean on your teen's strengths to fill the gaps between them (their weaker points, whether it be organisation or patience), rather than focusing on the gaps themselves. And sometimes those gaps can be blinding, so it requires a conscious decision and practice to do this.

To know your teen's strengths requires you to consider their whole person – what their natural talents and abilities are, as well as who they are and how they act in different situations. Being argumentative probably means they are able to think critically, but as parents we tend to get caught up in the argument rather than respecting the thought process behind it.

So spend time thinking about your teen's strengths – perhaps they're a great friend, so why can't they use those relationship strengths to be nicer to their brother? Or maybe they're really organised for sport, so why can't they organise their wardrobe so items can actually be found? Or if they are so persistent about English

homework, how can they use that for science?
Look at the strengths they have in some areas,
and see if they can be transferred to other areas.

The key benefit of strength-based parenting is
that a teenager who knows their strengths, and
is reminded of them, will have stronger self-worth,
and be more optimistic and resilient. Strengths are
not dependent on anyone else, either – they are
innate to the individual. A good example of a
strength here is kindness – someone who is kind is
kind to everyone, as opposed to just being nice to
the people they want to impress.

If you are looking for language around strength,
I strongly recommend the VIA character strengths
survey, which ranks our character strengths
from highest to lowest (my highest is bravery,
my lowest is patience ... which is a surprise to
literally nobody, I know).

So, although you get to see the worst of your
children, remember: they will only see the best
in themselves if you do.

8. What are your values?

When your teen was very young you probably started implementing some hard and fast rules. No TV after dark, or no dessert until you eat your vegetables. Say please and thank you. Don't scream. People are not for hitting.

When kids start getting a bit older, around six or seven, they really start questioning rules. 'I can watch TV after dark in winter, why does daylight savings change the rules?' or 'Why can't I yell? You're always yelling "dinner's ready".' or, my favourite, 'You can't get angry at me for forgetting where my shoes are when you can never remember where your car keys are.'

As children develop into teens they start to focus on the pernickety details of the rules rather than the 'spirit of the law', which is a point of optimism for future law firms but hell for parents.

To resolve this, one step I suggest is to move from rules to values.

There is a lot of research to support this idea. Psychologist Milton Rokeach created a value rating system that he named after himself, because, well, that's what he valued. His survey measures terminal values and instrumental values. Terminal values have to do with an ideal state of existence, and include things like happiness, equality and freedom. Instrumental values are around modes of behaviour, including cleanliness, self-control and obedience. So your instrumental values are the behaviours that will hopefully guide you to live a life that's aligned to your terminal ones. If you value freedom, for example, you would need to practise some self-control to be able to have freedom later in life. Or if you value happiness, then kindness might be the way to get there, because kindness nurtures healthy relationships and, as we know, relationships are the key to happiness.

Not to be outdone, professors Martin Seligman and Chris Peterson came up with the VIA (Values in Action) Character Strength Survey (which, frankly, I prefer, and deal in all the time), which has 24 values that are identified across cultures and eras. The VIA Survey states that everyone has all 24 character strengths, but in different weightings. You fill out a free survey online to find out your strengths in order.

Your top five are your signature strengths – they're you at your most you. Mine are bravery, industry, gratitude, kindness and honesty. There are no bad values, but they can have interesting combinations. For example, honesty is great – just don't ask me if you look fat in an outfit. I have also been known to overuse the character strength of bravery on occasion. I would share an example with you, but I'm not sure of the statute of limitations on throwing glitter into a convertible car that did not have a baby seat but was parked in the designated daycare spot in a shopping centre.

Other than getting your teenager to think of values rather than rules, and to save you many

APPRECIATION OF BEAUTY & ELEGANCE

BRAVERY

CREATIVITY

CURIOSITY

FAIRNESS

FORGIVENESS

GRATITUDE

HONESTY

HOPE

HUMILITY

HUMOUR

JUDGEMENT

KINDNESS

LEADERSHIP

LOVE

LOVE OF LEARNING

PERSEVERANCE

PERSPECTIVE

PRUDENCE

SELF REGULATION

SOCIAL INTELLIGENCE

SPIRITUALITY

TEAMWORK

ZEST

a courtroom argument, another reason why values are better than rules is that values can stay the same while the rules change. If you value kindness, then that could be sharing toys at age five. But as you get older, what defines kindness changes. To share your stuff is actually a lot easier to do – or at least, you can explain why you don't want to share a precious heirloom. But kindness can mean more, and can exist within and beyond rules.

Similarly, curiosity is a value I try to instil in my kids. Of course, as they get older that is going to bump heads with respect for privacy, which is another value I hold dear. But that's okay – we can manage that with some carefully established rules.

Values can also be used as boundaries in a non-judgemental way, whereas if you have certain rules and other people break them, this can lead you to judge their behaviour and fail to see any grey area in the way people act. You also run the risk of being a bit of a righteous ass. Far better to recognise you have different values.

Values also serve another great purpose. They can be a uniting force, helping to navigate individual differences. For example, if you live in a multifaith household, you can share the same values without necessarily having to debate religion. The same can apply in a multicultural family. The role of grandparents might be different between different cultures, but the shared values of respect and acceptance can help bridge the gaps. It is far easier to work in the value of 'love' than the rule of 'no lollies' – especially when one set of grandparents are vegan sugar-free and the other keep saying, 'You look so skinny, eat some chocolate!' (God I wish someone would tell me to eat some chocolate.)

And shared values between separated parents can be a lifesaver. You and your ex may have different rules about how you do specific things in your house, but the same overall values, which can help you establish some common ground without sweating the small stuff.

Values give us wriggle room while also being deeply rooted in our beings.

9. What are the consequences?

Responsibility and consequence need to be taught together. It is an innate thing for teenagers to be defensive when they are faced with a consequence. 'It wasn't me' or 'But they did it too' seem to be universal refrains from teenagers (and, unfortunately, some adults, too). They very rarely stop to reflect on how they got there. The opposite can also be true: guilt and shame can be another response to a consequence.

The goal here is to generate a healthy response to consequence. This comes from responsibility being developed over time as your teen gets older.

We make mistakes and there are consequences, and we learn from them. If the inability to fulfil a responsibility leads to a massive gap or loss, the responsibility is too large. But if the consequence has no impact, then the responsibility is too small.

Build them up slowly. One thing I often consider is that we trust 15- to 16-year-olds to babysit, but we haven't built them up to it with small responsibilities over time. The goal is fully functioning adults; the steps to that point should be so small that the path there looks more like an ancient cobbled Roman ramp than a box jump at each step.

Consequence and responsibility can also be developed through community. Now, we know that collective punishment, punishing the whole group for one's crime, doesn't work. But having authentic relationships and not wanting to let everyone down is a good motivator. Develop responsibilities that have communal consequences. No clean socks? It was Josie's job to do the laundry. Also, community is pro-social, and promotes positive behaviour and responsibility. This is of course highlighted in being a member of a sports team. Sure, you get sick or there are big events that mean you can't play ball, but it is a person of character who recognises the impact of not turning up to a game without a good reason.

There is also a conversation to be had around freedom and responsibility. Your teenager might want the freedom to not have to tell you exactly what they are up to, but that freedom has to be tied to a responsibility. Sure they can hang out with deadbeat Dave, but do you know they will call you when they need to, when things go really bad? Are they responsible enough to know when to do that?

10. What motivates you?

If you are reading this section, I'm guessing the issue is probably not that your teen is too motivated, although I have seen students put heaps of pressure on themselves. I remember sharing Sheryl Sandberg's line 'done is better than perfect' in a parent–teacher interview and the mother's face lighting up because someone else was telling her super-motivated daughter to cool it.

Motivation is a topic that has been extensively researched and discussed. There are two main areas of research I want to write about. The first is to do with professors Richard Ryan and Edward Deci's self-determination theory, which to me perfectly explains teenage motivation and how we can help them develop motivation. I touched on this in question 1 (page 42), but I want to go into the three key ideas in greater depth here:

1. Autonomy – how autonomous is your teen in the task? Is it something they have any choice in? If not, then this is not a great starting point for motivation, but that is also part of life. Autonomy relates to intrinsic and extrinsic motivation. Intrinsic motivation is when you are motivated to do the task on your own, because it brings you joy and/or you see a clear goal being achieved by completing the task. Extrinsic motivation is when external sources are pressuring you to complete the task.

Extrinsic motivation can be good, but it is best when it is reward- rather than punishment-focused. The best form of motivation is intrinsic and autonomous. One way to turn motivation from being extrinsic (do your Year 7 history homework) to intrinsic is to link it to a future goal (if you want to be a writer when you grow up, understanding sources and analysing them will be really important, so do your Year 7 history homework).

2. Competency – how well can your teen do the task? Video games are the perfect example of tasks that build on previous knowledge and challenge you that little bit more to feel a sense of achievement. And then 23 levels and eight hours later, you have no idea where the time went. This links into Mihaly Csikszentmihalyi's theory of flow. We achieve flow when there is a one-step challenge. To complete something that is way too difficult gives us anxiety, and to complete something really easy makes us bored. Competency is important, and achievement builds on achievement.

3. Relatedness – we as humans are motivated to be connected with others. We are more motivated when we feel we belong. Whether it is with the teacher or other students, we work so much more effectively when we feel we are part of a team. This can be hard to harness when so much of schooling is about rankings. Try to move away from that language with your teen and instead encourage them to look at the other students' strengths to learn from them, rather than confining themselves to always being 'dumber' than that kid. We know what it is like to work in a team we don't connect with or for a boss who doesn't respect us – it makes us less motivated. Relationships matter.

Of course, motivation is something that ebbs and flows, and we can't expect ourselves to be highly motivated all the time. Recognising how motivated we are on a certain day, or at a certain time of day, is very useful in knowing how best we work or do certain jobs. Motivation is also greatly affected by distraction, and there is nothing more distracting than the ping of a phone notification.

The song 'Hate Dah' by Super Silly has the line 'I roll my eyes when you text my phone ...' And boy isn't that the case with some people? But also, that dopamine hit we get from the ping, before we realise it's a text from someone eyeroll-worthy, is a serious thing. It disconnects us from a train of thought, a sentence, a maths problem. Now obviously the answer is to put your phone on silent and get back to it, right? In his book *Indistractable* Nir Eyal argues that what we actually need to look at is WHY we wanted to be distracted in the first place, and deal with that. Eyal argues that we have internal triggers that inspire traction (towards a goal) or distraction (away from a goal). We need to focus on the internal triggers – like having goals and a clear pathway to get there – that promote traction. Furthermore, Eyal encourages us to ask ourselves whether our external triggers are serving us, or whether we are serving them.

Say you are reading this book and at some point you pick up your phone. There is no message, there is no ping, you just stopped reading for some reason and picked up your phone. Eyal would argue that

there was some discomfort at play – boredom
(I really hope not!), difficulty, loneliness, feeling
overwhelmed, frustrated, nervous, anxious or
challenged. Once you realise you've picked up your
phone, ask yourself what you were actually feeling
right before you did so. As strange as it is to do, it
is helpful to know what internally distracts us.

(But while assessing your internal distractions,
may I also suggest turning off all notifications and
learning to embrace aeroplane mode at times?)

We need to talk to teenagers about the fact that
even though we are not always greatly motivated
to do something, we still have to do it. No teenager
wants to hear about how the annoying tasks at
school like group work and exams are 'actually
useful' for real life, but they really are, especially in
teaching kids that sometimes we just don't want
to do what we have to do. For me, it is writing
risk assessments (there's an irony there, I know).
But we have to do them. So, when faced with
something you really don't want to do, get it done
first, so it is done.

When we are talking about huge, overwhelming projects (like writing a book), it's a bit like eating an elephant – take it one bite at a time. Pick a daily goal and do that. Sometimes it will take all day, sometimes an hour. But stop when you reach your goal, and get ready to dig in again tomorrow.

Finally, let's talk about laziness. Professor Angela Duckworth, who I absolutely idolise, wrote the book *Grit*, which talks about that stickwithitness and persistence that successful people have, from writers to sportspeople and everyone in between. And in fact, she has made the point that it is okay for gritty people to be lazy at some things. You cannot do everything grittily, so if that means while you are studying really hard you aren't super motivated with other tasks, that is normal and okay.

But either way, we need to take responsibility for motivation. All of these hacks can help, but the most helpful thing is setting a goal and working towards it. That can be very difficult when the teenage years are often a time of figuring out, rather than being set in your ways. One of the easiest ways to consider a goal is to think back to your values – what could you do to help you achieve that value?

When talking to teenagers about motivation, this can also be an opportunity to discuss what motivates them socially. For example, I often see students getting kindness confused with niceness. Help your teen understand the difference between being nice due to a constant need to seek approval, as opposed to being kind, which is about who they are rather than who they are being kind to.

'If it's your job to eat a frog, it's best to do it first thing in the morning. And if it's your job to eat two frogs, it's best to eat the biggest one first.'

– MARK TWAIN

//. What do you do when you're bored?

Firstly, there is a great hypocrisy in me writing this, for I am absolutely shocking at being bored. But I know boredom can be the seed of creativity, as well as of depressive symptoms.

Teenagers hate boredom, but they're particularly likely to experience it. A Washington State University study in 2019 showed that in response to the statement 'I am often bored', the highest response for boys was in Year 10, so around 15–16 years old, and for girls was in Year 8, around 13–14. Boredom is an uncomfortable emotion for many. But it can be a good and necessary thing, and it's a 'problem' that we're often too quick to solve. In her book *Untamed*, author Glennon Doyle writes that when we throw phones at our kids, 'we steal their boredom from them'.

The ability to see an unscheduled day as an opportunity to sit and be bored, to problem-solve your way out of it, is a skill we need kids and teens to learn. Overscheduling to the point where you have no downtime gives you no chance to just sit with yourself. This is why it is important for your teen to have hobbies they can do on their own, be it crocheting, drawing, music, reading or model planes.

Boredom can be the seed of creativity, as well as its opposing force. The first byproduct of boredom is your mind wandering, which might turn into solving a problem. In fact, letting yourself get bored can be a form of percolation, rather than procrastination. We can use downtime to let our brain figure out what it wants to do next. This is why writers often spend a lot of time NOT writing, and are generally

quite hard to live with; it can seem like they have done nothing all day. That experience of boredom gives space for your mind to process everything it's been seeing, hearing and feeling, and start creating.

But boredom can also become a negative force in creativity. People who are chronically bored may be that way because they are stopping themselves from processing trauma, or it may be the result of avoidance due to anxiety. Boredom, at its heart, is about not being able to see novelty in daily life, which can lead people to engage in high-risk behaviours to seek adrenaline hits. If you observe this behaviour in your teen, think of ways to develop hobbies or healthy risks that they can undertake, without overscheduling them.

We want teenagers to be comfortable in their own skin, on their own. Teach your teen how to be bored, to savour it and do something with it. As with many things in life, it is about balance – in this case, the balance between an overscheduled co-curricular life and the constant refrain of 'I'm boooooored'.

12. How do you handle disappointment?

In *50 Risks*, I talked about the importance of letting young kids suck at something, so they know they are not brilliant at every single thing they do. Similarly, it's important for kids to learn how to handle disappointment. Being disappointed about something, be it big or small, is an experience you want your teen to have when they are still at home surrounded by loving parents.

You also want your teen to be able to recognise that the disappointment they may be feeling isn't always 'worthy' of disappointment. This helps them gain perspective. For example, if your teenager's biggest disappointment in life was not getting the latest iPhone for their birthday, that's not really an experience that's going to give them the skills to get through life. I am not suggesting you create some great tragedy just so your teen can tick the 'experience disappointment' box. But when they are faced with disappointment, resist the urge to step in and shield your teen from it.

The most important part of dealing with disappointment is sitting with it. Don't try to brush it away, or distract your teen from it with something new and shiny, or remind them of everything they have to be grateful for (not yet). The ability to sit with an uncomfortable emotion is a skill that a lot of adults could do with. I could do with it.

It is an uncomfortable fact that you can't actually get out of a painful emotion without processing it. Much like going on a bear hunt, you have to go through it. Remember, disappointment is an experience we all encounter at some point – many points – but it is one we grow through as well.

Let your teen see you be disappointed sometimes. Explain that this is a day when you will not be going at a million miles an hour, your usual services will not be provided tonight (dinner or homework assistance), that you need tea delivered to you, and that you will be fine in the morning. Model a healthy relationship with uncomfortable emotions.

Disappointment and failure are particularly difficult for teenagers who are perfectionists (the same is true of perfectionist adults). Perfectionism can be debilitating and sabotaging. The irony is, of course, that perfectionists will always be disappointed, because nothing and no one is perfect. They set themselves up for failure, and can experience disappointment over things that most people would see as a huge success. I wish I had better advice to give for perfectionism, but I keep going back to the very adamant value I was raised, and live, with: that I am not my work, that I am loved for who I am, and a mistake here and there, or a failed exam, isn't going to change that. If you asked my parents for their advice they would simply say, love your kids.

13. What brings you joy?

It's a big question for one with only four syllables. We all need joy in one way or another. For some, it can be incredibly easy to access; for others, the quest to find joy in small moments can be a painful reminder of the lack of it in their lives. During the COVID-19 pandemic there were a lot of memes. My favourite was a re-creation of the WWI recruitment poster 'And what did you do, Grandpa?' that had in Impact font 'I sent a lot of memes.'

Memes are stupid and fun, accessible and deep. They touch on different social issues and subcultures. My girlfriend Sabina has opened my eyes and my Insta stories to Soviet memes, which I love more than any normal person should.

The point is, they make us laugh, and that is exactly what we need sometimes, especially in the heaviest and darkest of times. We need moments of irreverence and joy. Is your teen someone who easily finds joy, or do they see themselves as far too deep and serious for such frivolity? What brings them joy?

I have split this section in two – for the silly teen and for the serious teen.

My teen is so silly

The silly teen will laugh at the stupidest of things. A Freudian slip in the classroom, a fart, the shock of a door opening in class setting off a chain of giggles no syllabus allows for. But these are moments of joy. And joy must be sought out in this world.

Silliness, and laughing at things, and stopping to smile, and finding contentment in moments of mundanity are often seen as signs not of joie de vivre but of stupidity. In our busy culture, we are often quick to dismiss a giggle as not being serious enough. But what is wrong with joy? Why not come at life like a child when the world tells us there is so much badness? Does laughing at a meme change the nature of what is being laughed at?

My point is this: There are huge psychological benefits to seeking and enjoying joy. People who are able to seek joy, awe and wonder are happier, healthier and have more friends. It is far easier to be resilient when you can laugh, both at yourself and at life.

So don't dismiss giggles as silliness, but rather share in joy when it is seen and experienced. There is more than enough time to be serious.

My teen is so serious

There is nothing wrong with a serious teen – let's face it, there's a lot to be serious about. But there is definitely something to be said for joy, and finding moments of it.

The serious teen is not necessarily incapable of experiencing irreverent moments of joy, but their expression of it may be, as with many things, more demure.

There is no KPI for joy. But there is a great benefit in being able to experience it, and seek it out. It is a skill to be cultivated rather than a box to tick. To think of ways to seek out joy, you need to think like a child. But if your teen is past the point of enjoying crabs scuttling or clouds forming, the skill may need to be rehoned.

Learning to appreciate beauty and savour happy moments is one strategy to develop this skill. There is a lot of research into how to savour joy, but the Greater Good Institute at Berkeley University in California suggests:

1. Sharing your good feelings with others – tell people when you have enjoyed something. As parents, this could be fostered by asking your teen what good things happened, or hunting for the good stuff.
2. Taking a mental photograph – try to focus on positive things when you are on a walk or having a good day at school.
3. Getting absorbed in the moment – leave your phone at home and allow yourself to get in a state of flow.

14. Who are you online?

One day, I bumped into a local politician I know.
I asked if I could 'be a constituent for a minute', and
said I didn't agree with the fact that he sometimes
picked fights with people on Twitter. He said it was
just Twitter, and what you say on Twitter doesn't
really matter. I said I disagreed, and that who you
are online is who you are. He also disagreed, adding
'thanks for the feedback'.

Let me make this very clear – I think he is wrong.
I believe that who you are online is who you are.
To be an authentic human, you cannot act one way
on one medium and another way on another. You
might show different aspects of yourself on different
platforms – for example, your profile picture on a
dating app might be very different from the one
you use on LinkedIn – but who you are should be
the same, and it should reflect the real you.

Now, I am 36(ish). I have said some stupid things in group chats, and my first few years of Facebook statuses tried way too hard to play in the third person. But I try very hard to be myself online. And it is HARD to be yourself when you don't know who the real you is yet. Parents are often flabbergasted at what their kid might post, but often their teen may not know why they've done it.

From someone who has worked hard not to embarrass her family, from her teens through to her thirties, here are my tips for teens for keeping themselves nice online:

1. Call your grandma and check if what you're about to post shocks her.

2. Imagine seeing what you've written on the cover of the newspaper.

3. Test it out on friends (one friend of mine always calms my tweets down, the other always makes them more incensed).

4. Keep your group chats clean or incredibly trusting. There should be a clear relationship between how much you trust the people in your group chat and how honest and inappropriate you are willing to be.

5. Agree to a semi-regular wipe of group chat content because, let's face it, sometimes jokes age poorly.

There is something that strips away inhibitions while texting. You say things you would not say in person. In relationships I think this goes even further. The majority of flirting and dating is happening online, over text, where we become less inhibited than we would be in person. Our shyness around what we see in someone we like is protected by the keyboard, the screen, the radio waves between your screen and theirs, their keyboard, their eyes.

We see this in the comments sections of news articles and group chats, and we see it in courtship as well. People are far more likely to be opinionated, aggressive and inappropriate online than they would be in person. It's too easy to become a keyboard warrior, and to forget that the person you are interacting with is still, well, a person, not just an avatar or an anonymous account.

I had a text conversation about sex with a guy I was dating. It started due to a confusing use of an emoji (his, not mine). Overall, it was a great chat, despite starting strangely. I could type things I could not say. I never picked it up again in person though, so it was this one conversation in a parallel relationship. I wish I had brought the strands together; I shall blame my generation.

There is an aggression and a lack of inhibition online, but also a risk. It is important to know the people you talk to, and to always remember that, as the great *New Yorker* cartoon says, 'On the internet, nobody knows you're a dog'.

There is not much today that teens do not share online. They are tapped into social media, which would be fine if they were just sharing pasta recipes and crochet patterns, but what they see is more extreme, and it's becoming normalised. These days, normal for teens includes hypersexualised images, violence, derogatory language and disrespect.

The privacy conversation can happen early. It should absolutely happen before your kids go on social. Aristotle once referred to the play *Oedipus Rex* as having unity of place because it existed in a liminal space – literally the threshold between public and private. This is a good way to describe the grey area between private and public to teens. There is the private sphere of family, and the public out there, but it's important to recognise that there is a space between the two, where people can see in. How much of their lives do they want to be in that space?

Also talk about family privacy when your teen starts posting. You may not want identifiable images of your home, or the fact that you are away from home, being shared online (an invite for burglars). You can start seeking their consent to post images of your teen online, and expect the same of images they post of you. Promote the use of close friend circles on social media apps, as well as private accounts.

In romantic relationships I think the implications of being online go even further. Talking to your teen about sending nudes is going to be uncomfortable for both of you, but it is still a conversation you need to have. This goes back to freedom and consequence (question 9, page 88). Don't send nudes to someone who is harassing or pressuring you to do so. If they call you a prude, fine. It is far better to be a prude than to share something and regret it. Again, go back to whether or not you want it on the cover of the newspaper – or coming up in a job interview.

Now might also be a good time to just remind them that anything they put online will be there forever and could affect future career options (especially in politics).

/5. How do you manage conflict?

We cannot escape disagreements in life, and nor should we want to. Teenagers are particularly ready to argue, and it's a skill they need to learn, whether it is in the workplace, over lunch with extended family, or with a best friend or a partner. It's important to remember that two things are happening when teens argue – one, their prefrontal cortex is going absolutely berserk because it isn't fully developed, so they are probably saying some things they haven't really thought through. Secondly, they are learning on the job.

Teenagers need to experience good arguing. Sadly, many of them only see what bad arguing looks like. Now, this is not a moment for me to talk about marriage or role modelling, because I am not particularly good at either, but talking to your teen about how to argue respectfully will be very useful and significant for them growing up. This is another of those things that we just assume teens will learn via osmosis, rather than needing to be taught.

If you are arguing with a person, it is because you care enough about them, and the topic you are arguing over, that you cannot just walk away from it. So the most important thing to remember in an argument is that the other person wants to be heard – that's why they are talking so much or so loudly. It is important to hear them and not just jump into the holes in their argument or become defensive, tempting as that can be. You need to pause after they have spoken and say something

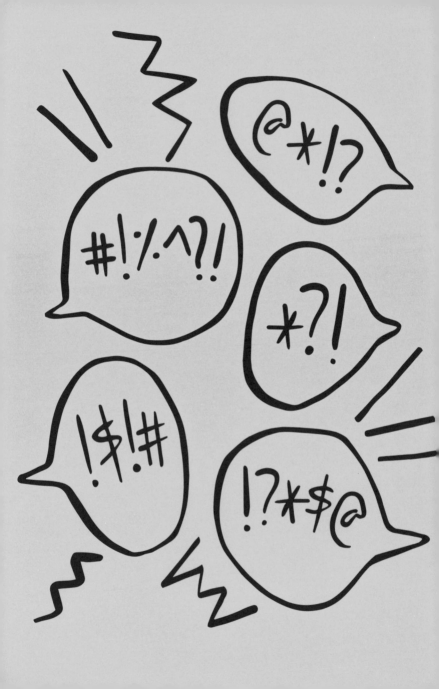

that shows you've understood this. For example, 'You're really upset about this' or 'I hear you are angry that I ...' Doing this means you are both speaking the same language.

It is normal and, as I said, easy to get defensive. Your teen has every right to defend themself in an argument, but make sure they know to do so in a way that doesn't attack the other person. This is why 'I' statements are far more useful in an argument than 'you' statements. 'I feel ...' is going to get you somewhere. 'You always ...' is going to get you back on the hamster wheel of conflict.

Tell your teen there is nothing wrong with deferring an argument until both people are both less angry. Saying you need time to think and going for a walk for 10 minutes can make a huge difference. Just make sure you don't spend that time formulating new arguments to beat them. Think about what is important here – the relationship.

Finally, if your teen finds themself having the same arguments with the same person all the time, suggest they give those arguments a name – it might be competition, it might be jealousy. Little arguments about not emptying the dishwasher, or a friend not waiting after class are not actually about dishwashers or classes, they're about the thread of discontent that runs through the relationship. Being able to name the problem means you can address the actual problem, rather than the symptoms. Deal with that, when you're both calm.

Boundaries are really important in arguments. You get to set your own boundaries, and you have to communicate them. It may be that you won't be sworn at – that is one of mine. As soon as someone starts swearing at me, I say 'I won't be spoken to this way' and hang up the phone or walk away. People who know me know that I swear, but never in arguments. Because for me, not swearing is about being in control of my emotions, and when I can see that someone is not in control of their emotions, I know there is no benefit in continuing the argument. Your boundaries might develop around time, or places. Set them, enforce them, and encourage your teen to do the same.

'We have friends for a reason, friends for a season, and friends for life.'

– INTERNET-ICISED FROM ARISTOTLE

Relating

We are social animals, made to relate to others – and relationships do not mean just sexual partners. You are in a relationship with everyone you know – whether it is familial, working, platonic or romantic. You cannot escape other humans, and if you intend to, this book is not for you or your teen.

This section is not just about sexual relationships, though there are some questions that are very much about them, or that apply to them. I joke that those questions should be in a sealed section – 'break in case of sexually active teen' – but the fact is, they need to be discussed whether your teen is sexually active or not.

We know that relationships are the single biggest factor in a person's happiness, and we know that people with good relationships (and not just with their partners) live longer.

We also know that in 2020 (and 2021), COVID-19 shut people off from most of their relationships, and that teenagers were the group that appeared to be most affected by this. We still do not know what the impact of those lockdowns will be on teenagers, but if they have missed anything from losing a few months to over a year of normal relations, it is even more important to talk to them.

Our relationships are dependent on how we feel about ourselves, and about others. For that reason, some of these questions are not directly about relationships or friendships, but about the fact that what we feel and the way we behave impact not only ourselves but also those around us.

16. What makes a good friend?

Everyone wants their teen to have friends, but it would be naive to suggest that the concept of friendships does not cause parents stress. We worry that our teens will choose the 'wrong' friends, or won't have 'enough' friends, or will have 'too many' friends, or will 'only care' about their friends. You might have visions of your teen staying friends with the children of the parents you met when they were a baby, but that's just not how these things work. So let's look at what you can actually do to be helpful here, because we know teens need peers (you know, in case you are eaten by mammoths and they only have people their own age left).

As a parent, you need talk to your teen directly about why we need good friends and about whether their friends are fulfilling that need, and encourage your teen to be a good friend to others.

You should be doing two things with your teen.

1. Asking what they look for in a friend and how they are there for their friends.
2. Finding out WHO they go to. Be genuinely interested, because these people are going to be in your teen's life for a while. Ask for names, and look and laugh at photos. Be as included as your teen wants you to be, and appreciate that they are sharing their new connections with you.

This conversation around who your teen hangs out with will then lead to some further conversations around what makes a healthy friendship and what makes an unhealthy one. Do not back away from these conversations, but rather see them as an opportunity to expand your teen's social skills.

We can be so focused on keeping relationships that may not be good for us, or may not be good for us forever. Friendships can end or fade away for a multitude of reasons, and while there can be grief in any relationship ending, this is also an opportunity to talk to your teen about what may have been healthy, or unhealthy, in that relationship. Learning to develop healthy relationships is often about understanding who we are in those relationships. If you notice your teen is always the friend making the effort, ask them why they think that is. If you notice that your teen seems to be burning through friends, talk about that as well.

Finally, get them to actually call their friends, or to see them in person. So much confusion happens over text. During lockdown we realised how much more connected we felt after talking on the phone (or dare I say, Zoom), instead of just texting back and forth.

Another reason to talk to your teen about the value of friendships is so that when they find themselves in a romantic relationship, they understand why it's important to maintain their friendships too.

My parents met each other and fell in love when Dad was 23 and Mum was 19. They have been together for over 40 years. They are best friends, utterly in love with each other, and they have built an amazing life, family and friendship together. However, a love story like that is not everyone's.

My marriage ended in 2020 and, incredibly sad as the experience was, I know I would not have gotten through it all if not for my family and friends. I only have those relationships because I have worked at them. There were times I felt myself disappearing into my relationship, but my friends kept me grounded.

Women who lose touch with their friends while in a romantic relationship are particularly at risk. It's an

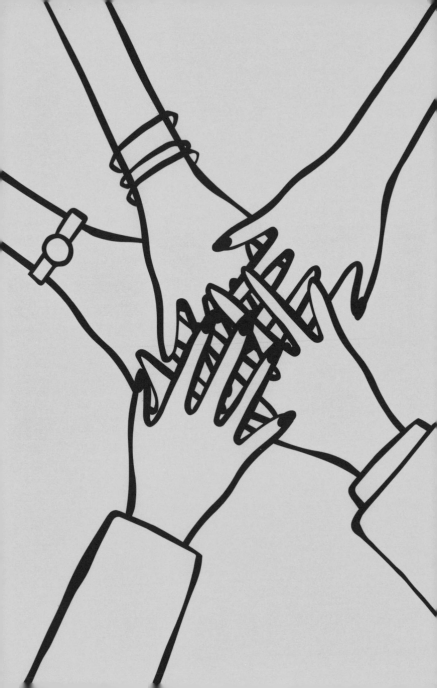

extreme example, but one of the first tricks in the domestic violence playbook (which I discuss more in question 19, page 148) is to try to isolate a partner from their networks and family.

As parents of teenagers, it's important to discuss how romantic relationships are great, and are healthy, but to emphasise that what's even more important are the relationships that sustain you beyond and outside infatuation and a little bit of under-the-sweater action.

Teach your teen, especially boys, to respect the friendships their partner has. No one person can meet all of another person's needs, and nor should they want to – it's an impossible task. Friendships will sustain them alongside relationships. They are not relationships to be jealous of, but ones that contribute to their world.

Teach your teen to respect their own friendships – they might be the longest and most significant relationships of their life.

/7. **What's really going on?**

As parents, there are things that happen every day, and they affect us differently. Think about decomposing bananas in school bags, for example. Some days you pull a decomposing banana out of a school bag and roll your eyes and throw it in the bin. Other days, you get furious, call the owner of said school bag into the kitchen and make them do chores to make up for the state of both the bag and the banana – and, frankly, for the state you're in too.

The problem is though, you are not actually angry about the banana. It's not about the banana at all. It is all about the state in which you enter the banana situation. If you are relaxed and you have had a very effective day and you feel like you have achieved a lot and are ready for a lovely time with your family after school, then you will not care about the banana. If you are stressed and your boss has been at you all day, not to mention the kids not being helpful in the morning, not to mention the dog needs to go to the vet, then you will absolutely blow your lid over a decomposing banana.

On a stressed-out day, if the banana didn't exist, the same reaction would be triggered by a scrunched-up note about homework or another call from work or a snarky refusal to help tidy up after dinner. Something would have made you blow.

In fact, what we need to understand is the concept of priming that leads up to anger. In his book *Resilient*, Rick Hanson talks about the importance of understanding the mood we are in and why. How stressed are you before you enter a situation that may or may not be stressful? It is important to act in proportion to the trigger (the banana) rather than in proportion to all of the priming that has occurred that day (the stress, the boss, the dog). Because when we get disproportionately angry at our teens, they learn to react that way as well.

The same works for when your teen gets angry about something – you will know, because they'll often make statements that start with 'You never …' or 'You always …', even though you probably do, most of the time do, or don't, as the case may be. Ask them what is actually going on. Why has this pretty innocuous event led to such a reaction? What's happening today? How stressed were they before they reached their trigger? Ask them how bad the trigger/event actually is, and how highly primed they are to react to it.

If the trigger event really is big, then of course your teen can get angry about it, but make sure you set clear boundaries about what anger can look like in your family. No swearing, no hitting, no destruction of property are pretty easy rules to stick to. But even a really big let-down (like, our

entire lives being cancelled because of COVID-19)
can be discussed calmly, when the priming is
healthy and well thought-out.

Remember, ultimately, it is rarely about the banana.

18. What are your boundaries?

Shortly after my marriage ended, I was talking to a girlfriend, who, like many, was in shock. She told me I must have had too many walls and not enough windows in my marriage. As much as I would like to credit her with this idea, it was coined by the psychologist Shirley Glass. The idea is simple – in any relationship there are walls between you as a couple and the outside world. The windows in those walls are what you let in and out. Too many windows and a marriage is easily susceptible to infidelity and breakdown. But not enough windows can be unhealthy, too.

The funny thing is that in myself, I am all windows. I love and trust and overshare. But I know the boundaries. Growing up, it was about never wanting to embarrass my parents. As a mother, it is about not wanting to embarrass my kids, but it's also about sharing our lives with those we trust.

It all comes back to boundaries. I have seen so many students get caught up in the lives of others, wanting to fix their friends' and partner's problems. This comes from love, but it also comes from not understanding their own personal boundaries.

We need to make sure teenagers understand the concept of boundaries so they are able to protect themselves and respect others.

The term 'boundaries' was once probably only discussed in cognitive behaviour therapy sessions, but has since leaked into our common language. Many adults discover, when learning about boundaries, that the issues they have with their mother-in-law, oldest school friend, or even their partner, stem from their own lack of boundaries. This is why it's important to talk to teenagers about boundaries. This one comes with a caveat, though – they may realise they can set boundaries with you as well. While this may seem strange at first, trust me, it's a good thing.

A boundary at its simplest separates you from others, physically, psychologically or emotionally. It can be as simple as the boundary of time – you have time that you spend with family or friends, and that time is sacrosanct. Or you have a boundary around intimacy. Boundaries can very much be in the back of your mind until they are pushed.

A boundary does not mean you have no vulnerability or ability to connect with people. Boundaries are also not designed to be used in manipulative ways. That being said, the stronger the relationship, the less the need to talk about boundaries.

As a parent, you want your teen to have good boundaries. Part of parenting teenagers is handing over the responsibility you have for them – to them. Boundaries are about self-control. They are not about a third party who might come up against the boundary, like a hiker stumbling across a fence they did not expect to see. They are about the person who built the fence. You are not telling other people how to behave; instead, you are setting rules or values around how you will be treated. Have clear boundaries around what is and is not acceptable behaviour. Being sworn at. Being stood up. Encourage your teen to decide what they will tolerate and what they will not. And empower them to hold that line.

Boundaries will test some relationships, but they will strengthen many more. When you have boundaries, you can manage all aspects of your life, from your time to your relationships.

A lot of romantic films present humans as incomplete puzzle pieces desperately seeking someone to 'fit'. This is not an anti-love rant, but it is important to be firm in ourselves and in our own integrity, our character, so that we can remain ourselves within relationships, while also being honest and vulnerable. Boundaries remind us who we are. They link to other questions of values and peer pressure. But the discussion and acknowledgement of boundaries means that we are able to recognise the need to tend to our own gardens before we start trying to cross-pollinate. Boundaries teach us how to understand and respect our own needs, and how to be respectful and understanding of the needs of others.

And remember, if your teen has been clear in their boundaries, and spoken to people who may be upsetting them, and those people continue to push those boundaries, make sure your teenager knows they can talk to you about it.

Boundaries can be physical:

- asking friends or family not to come around unexpectedly
- respecting private spaces like bedrooms
- around sex and relationships.

Boundaries can also be communicative. You can communicate when:

- something someone has said to you has upset you
- you don't like the way someone communicates with you
- you may not want to participate in bitching or badmouthing.

Boundaries can be emotional:

- asking for space when you feel your boundaries have been pushed
- saying that you feel a certain way, using 'I' statements, rather than blame-driven 'you' statements
- having a boundary with yourself that requires you to sit with an emotion rather than doing anything with it.

19. What does control mean?

Each week in Australia, a woman is killed by a current or past domestic partner. Domestic violence is not always physical violence, and it is less and less likely to be. The silent killer in Australia (and globally) is coercive control in relationships. Defining coercive control is difficult because, although it very much fits a pattern, it presents a slightly different experience for every victim. In Australia the government is trying to criminalise coercive control, and has created this definition: 'patterns of abusive behaviour designed to exercise domination and control over the other party in a relationship'. But there is concern that this definition can be misunderstood.

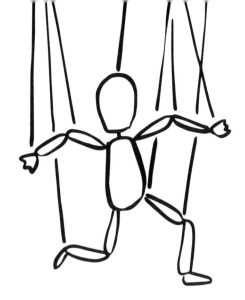

I would love to say this is not an issue teenagers need to worry about, because clearly they're not living with their partners – but, in fact, girls aged 16–25 are the group at the highest risk of being victims of coercive control. So let's talk about it – with both our daughters and our sons, because anyone can be a victim of coercive control, and many people who do control their partners don't know they are doing it.

Jess Hill, in her book *See What You Made Me Do* (which I implore you all to read), wrote that one of the most shocking things survivors say when coming out of coercive control relationships is how it all happened like it came out of 'the perpetrator's handbook'. As though the steps are written down on a scrap of paper for perpetrators to hand to each other, memorise and enact. Coercive control, in fact, is not passed on through generations but built into our identity and the problems with masculinity in our society at this very long moment.

These are the red flags young people need to be aware of in any relationship (and parents, too):

LOVE BOMBING

Love bombing goes beyond infatuation and flowers. It is an intensity in affection that moves incredibly quickly. The 'I love you's flow. There is so much love, so much affection, that you feel incredibly adored and whole with this person. While there can be other indicators and red flags, this one, when done well, can camouflage all the others. In fact, this first step in coercive control is what victims think back to longingly in rationalising later behaviour, saying to themselves, and to others, 'It wasn't always like this, they used to be so loving, I'm sure it will sort out soon.' Victims tend to yearn for a return to this first step when things get bad.

ISOLATION FROM FRIENDS AND FAMILY

This is where a strong relationship with your teen is so important. If your connection is based on strong foundations, it is harder for your teen to be isolated. Isolation doesn't just come in the form of 'your mum is a whackjob, I don't want to have lunch with your family today'. It might be that the partner makes it difficult for your teen to see their friends. They might say your teen's friends don't mesh well with theirs, for whatever reason. They might say a friend should be a 'solo friend' who your teen sees on their own, and then ensure there is never time to see them. Conversely, they may try to take over friendships by asking to be included in group chats, then trying to stop that friendship from continuing except under their eye. This happens slowly. It happens incrementally, and the victim is the frog in the pot. They do not realise they are being boiled.

As relatives and friends of people in controlling relationships, the absolute worst thing we can do is let them be isolated. That is doing the perpetrator's job for them. Ever said, or heard someone else say, 'Yeah, but she's got a new boyfriend and I don't really like the guy'? It is as old as time. Don't shut doors to people you think might be in controlling relationships.

CONTROLLING MOVEMENTS

Some might think that when your teen is living in your house, controlling movements might be a bit, er, boring, but a lot of this happens online. Checking when someone has been online on a chatting/social media app, or getting alerts whenever they tweet or post online are forms of surveillance that can tell someone exactly what another is doing. This can then lead to having clear data that can be used in arguments, and to gaslighting (see page 156) – 'I know you were online because I saw you post on Instagram at 3 pm, but you didn't reply to my message at that time, so clearly you're having an affair'. The victim is then on the back foot, forced

to justify not responding to a text, which then establishes the power balance for the rest of that day or a longer period of time. Apps such as Find My iPhone or Find My Friends are often used by girls to check their friends are okay when they are out, and I have not been on a first or second date without sharing my live location with a friend. But these apps that are designed to keep us safe can also keep us very controlled.

INVASIONS OF PRIVACY

Invasions of privacy can go hand in hand with controlling someone's movements. They can also be part of love bombing. 'He likes me so much he wants us to share our locations with each other.' Again, a lot of this is much easier to do online than it was 30 years ago, and is becoming even more so. Sometimes this is perpetrated in ways that can appear coincidental, such as becoming friends with your friends, or finding new points of contact that embed the person in your life further.

FINANCIAL CONTROL

Financial control is not hugely likely in the teenage years but, to prevent it from occurring down the track, it's important to talk to your teen about developing financial independence. Be sure both members of a couple are equally transparent with each other about finances. As your teen might move into a more serious and 'adult' relationship, including moving in with their partner, have conversations with them around their own financial independence, and being honest about any debt they and their partner might have.

HUMILIATING/DEGRADING BEHAVIOUR

This is generally the first red flag anyone sees, but it happens quite far down the line. This might be a joke at your expense, references to weight or intellect – and these are the ones that happen in public. Remember, what happens in public is often a tenth of what happens in private. In positive psychology it is often said that it takes five positive comments to make up for each negative one. If your partner is making one or two negative comments a day – small niggles or 'jokes' – you'll be like a heat-seeking missile for compliments. You may also return to the person who insulted you to find those compliments. This can be the foundation of gaslighting (see below). In the case of degrading comments, the gaslighting will be something along the lines of 'Why are you always looking for validation? You are so high maintenance.' This can take an enormous toll. When someone is no longer receiving a daily put-down, they start to recognise compliments as the mood-boosting gift they are meant to be, rather than emotional Spakfilla.

GASLIGHTING

This is when someone makes you question your own reality, and makes you think there must be something wrong with you rather than something wrong in your relationship with them. For example, your partner might deny that something happened, even though you know it did, or say that you are imagining something that you know was real. This can then lead to you thinking that you are lucky to be with the person, who still loves you despite your own insecurities (that they created). This will also lead to a huge amount of rationalisation, and wishing the relationship could go back to how it was (during the love bombing, which we know was all part of the process).

THREATS AND MANIPULATION

Threats and manipulation are often used by teenagers. I have heard students speak about how partners or friends have threatened to spill a huge secret, hurt themselves or kill themselves if their partner doesn't do what they ask or doesn't agree to stay with them. I have heard parents say they know these threats are generally bluffs, but that their teen is scared about them, and rightly so. These are scary things to go through. When I was a teenager I received a threatening letter from a boyfriend saying he would kill himself if I didn't stay with him. The moment I told my parents about it, a weight lifted because they knew exactly what to do. If your teen ever communicates that they are receiving threats or manipulative texts, let them know there will be no judgement, and that you are there to support them. A lot of this will happen online. If you are aware that your teen is receiving any threats, you have several options, including confronting the family of the perpetrator if you know them, working within and between the schools, or talking to the cops. You have more control of this situation than you may think. It does not escalate beyond your control as quickly as you might expect.

PHYSICAL VIOLENCE AND DESTRUCTION OF PROPERTY

This can happen in all types of relationships. With physical violence, which is often a part of coercive control, there is almost always a cycle of violence. At first everything is fine, and then there is a build-up and the victim starts feeling like they are walking on eggshells. Eventually there will be a crisis stage, with a lashing out or episode of physical violence. This will very quickly be followed by a great apology, then, in what's known as the honeymoon phase – the love bombing starts all over again.

It is important to remember that with a lot of these steps, victims think they *want* to do the things they are doing, like sharing their location or not seeing their friends, because they have been coerced into it, or because it is easier not to have the fight. They cannot tell you the moment they decided to share all their passwords with their partner, because that moment never happened – it was a mutual decision.

If you think your teen is in an unhealthy relationship, then the question to ask them is this: 'How would your partner feel if they knew we were having this conversation?' After more than three years at Lifeline, I can tell you the answer is never 'They'd be fine with it.' Once your teen has admitted the relationship is unhealthy, you can start planning with them.

There are multiple resources available online if you need them. I hope you never do, but one in four women aged over 15 have experienced physical or sexual violence at the hands of a partner, so there is a real chance that your teen, or a friend of theirs, will go through this.

20. What is your relationship with porn?

I thought long and hard about how to write this question, because porn impacts people in different ways. I also didn't want to make it about gender. So instead, I have structured it into two sections: the gazer and the gazed upon. Huzzah, that gender studies major paid off!

But firstly, let's look at some stats on porn. Porn is everywhere online and your teenager has very likely seen it, as most kids have by the age of 11. That is not your fault. Porn is a bit like swearwords; all it takes is for one kid at school to have an older sibling and then the whole playground is effectively 'levelled up'.

Porn is easily accessible, and it is not going anywhere. It is changing sexual appetites. A kid who starts watching pretty normal porn will get desensitised, or tolerant, to it and then will seek out more porn, or new genres of porn, which almost always means more violent and dominating porn. Porn interests escalate. If your teenager starts watching some risqué series or French movies on SBS when they are 13, then by the time they're 16 or 17 they'll be watching pretty hardcore porn. As I explained to some friends once, it's a bit like *Game of Thrones*. That first season we were all 'ahh blood, murder, thrown off a wall, raped, this is too much', but then by the final season we're all 'yeah a whole city was just burnt by a dragon and someone was raped, not much happened'.

Porn can affect people in two different ways: either by watching it, or by interacting with others who do. Therefore, talking to your teen about porn requires two conversations:

The gazer

If your teen is watching porn as the gazer, then you need to tell them that porn is not real. It is not how sex between most people is, and it is certainly not the kind of sex teenage girls expect, or want to be having. Don't get judgemental about the fact they're watching porn, but ensure the reality of the situation is clear.

The biggest issue with teenage boys watching porn seems to be that they consider porn sex to be sexy and everything else to be boring. But even more, in an *Atlantic* article in 2018 on the teenage sex recession, we learned that teen boys are having less sex and some aren't even bothering with dating because it's too hard – all that effort, and then the sex doesn't live up to their expectations. Teenage boys are having issues with erectile dysfunction from the dissociative experience of watching porn, which also perpetuates the myth that 'men are rock hard and women are ready for sex all the time', says Clare Faulkner, a psychosexual and relationship counsellor.

So, maybe you walk in on your son watching porn and have a preemptive chat, or maybe they're already facing these issues. Either way, it's important to ensure they understand that porn isn't real, and that it creates unrealistic expectations.

It used to be that you'd start feeling sexual in your mid-teens and then have sex and then maybe start watching porn. Now porn is the start of it, and teens are watching it before they are sexually aware, which means it is guiding sexual appetites. Porn is how a lot of teens are introduced to sex. It is forming their sexual identity. But furthermore, as Dr Lisa Damour discusses in her podcast, *Ask Lisa*, your teen creates a link between watching porn – which they know is wrong, so they feel shame – and having a physical response to it. This starts to build a cognitive link between sex, pleasure and shame.

The gazed upon

Unless your partner tells you that they watch a lot of porn, you only know your partner watches a lot of porn when it infiltrates your sex life. There is no laughter or playfulness, oral sex becomes about power instead of enjoyment, and there is a lot of stuff happening from behind. There is also an expectation that women will orgasm in an instant.

It can be hard to realise that this is not about you, but it isn't. If your teenager is the gazed upon, the conversation you need to have is about the importance of open communication and boundaries around sex. They need to tell their partner that they want sex to be different from how it is, and to be about both their enjoyment. This might lead to the relationship ending, to a lot more conversations, and potentially even some shame, but these outcomes are all better than having bad sex for the rest of your life.

This is also specifically difficult for females who may know nothing about sex, meaning they can't suggest anything else. This pairing of bad knowledge against almost no knowledge leaves little space for talking about what each other wants. So, if you are comfortable talking to your teenager about sex and pleasure, talk about it with them honestly. If you are not, due to any number of reasons, from awkwardness to religious and cultural beliefs, be honest with them about that. Explain that you don't want to have the conversation, but that you understand and support them if they want to discuss it with another trusted adult or friend.

There is nothing wrong with watching some porn, but it can't be the standard all sex is set to. There is also porn for women that focuses on female pleasure. Talk about porn, because it is definitely having an influence.

Note: I structured and wrote this section in a very heteronormative way, because that is what I've mainly experienced in my teaching and research. But the gender of the gazer and the gazed upon can be interchangeable, and if you want more information specifically on LGBTQIA+ teen areas, see page 343 of the resources section.

21. **What do you know about consent?**

The topic of consent is one that really should be pretty simple, and yet over and over again we read stories of rape, sexual assault and harassment.

Consent is actually something that can be discussed from a surprisingly early age. I considered including it in *50 Risks*, but I think age 10 is really when you want to start having the conversation.

You probably don't want to have 'the talk' about sex when your kid is 'too young', but remember, the majority of 11-year-olds have seen porn. Sex is out there. Talk to your teen about sex before someone else shows them a very different idea of what it is.

I remember very distinctly having two talks. The first was about how stuff works. Periods, ovulation, sperm, pregnancy. I think I was about 11.

The second talk was a few years later. It probably coincided with a boy's name being mentioned a few times and Mum and Dad thinking they should update the talk in the context of me actually having sex. I remember Mum kept saying I had to feel comfortable. More on that later.

I don't think we had the third talk – the 'consent' talk. Maybe we did. But I think because Mum really reminded me over and over about being comfortable, the concept of not being comfortable, and that not being okay, was clearly implied. It was there, it just had a different language.

Today you need to do all three talks in one, and the consent part of the conversation needs to come up again and again, and again.

THE TALK

- You need to explain how stuff works. You need to cover the actual birds and the bees. This can include contraception, depending on your family's views.

- If your family believes sex is only for after and within marriage, then explain why.

- Don't make sex scary or shameful. In every religion and culture, it is okay to enjoy it. There is nothing wrong about sex.

- Explain that while sex is meant to be enjoyed, it can take a while to get to that point, and that's okay.

- Introduce the idea of consent. Explain that when it comes to sex, your teen should only ever do what they want, what they feel comfortable with. Nobody who loves or cares about them would coerce, bully, guilt trip or force them into doing anything they don't feel comfortable with. Tell your teen to tell their partner that anything but an enthusiastic yes is a no.

- Also explain that while there is never any excuse for consent not being sought and respected, your teen can protect themself by avoiding getting stupidly drunk and by always being with friends who they trust and who won't leave them on their own. (But that's a conversation about alcohol in general.)

- Explain that what your teen sees with porn is not what sex is like, and to be careful watching it. Tell them that if they are not absolutely certain their partner wants to have sex, if there is a not an enthusiastic yes in the moment, then it is a no. Explain that they cannot get resentful if their partner doesn't want to have sex – there will be other times (and that this is more likely if they treat people with respect!).

- Also tell your teen that while it may be the 'done thing' to boast about sex, it is far better to be discreet than to brag.

- Tell your teen that drunk people are never consenting. Passed-out people are never consenting. Tell them to tell their friends, too.

- Tell them to always use protection. Even if you do not support premarital sex, but you think your teen is having sex, ensure they are being safe.

- The rules around consent are exactly the same for people in relationships as for those engaging in 'hookups'.

AND ANOTHER TOPIC – WHERE?

Look, if your teen is having sex and you don't like it, that ain't going to stop them. Teens who can't have partners over go and have sex in stupid places, and sometimes get caught by the police. My grandmother, who grew up in the 1940s, once told me she and her 'friend' would swim into Sydney Harbour and use empty moored sailing boats. Kind of genius, and totally stupid. Just remember, before you say 'no sex here', think about where else they're going to go.

Judgement shuts doors. Don't shut doors on this stuff.

'Thank God he didn't rape you'

The first people girls go to when they feel something has happened to them are their girlfriends. Brent Sanders, an ex–police officer and expert on workplace harassment and sex crimes, says that when girls describe things like being digitally penetrated or being talked or forced into giving oral sex, their friends will respond with, 'That's terrible, but at least he didn't rape you.' Teach your daughter (and son) that sexual assault is defined as penetration to a sexual area with anything, including forced oral sex – it doesn't just mean sex without consent. Make sure they know this, so that if a friend ever confides in them, they know what is sexual assault/rape.

'She was into it'

There is a joke in the Monty Python film *The Life of Brian* where Brian incredulously asks his mother if she was raped, and she responds that she was at first. A lot of young men think that multiple 'no's eventually followed by a 'yes' is consent. It is not; it is coercion. In fact, the definition of consent in multiple jurisdictions does not mention the word 'yes'. It does, however, mention the word 'freely'. Consent has to be given freely. One of the most concerning things about the 'field theory' that the Australian Government based its 2021 consent program on was that there is a 'yes zone', a 'maybe zone' and a 'no zone'. Some of the videos (which were promptly removed) suggested that one could be moved from the no zone, through the maybe zone and into the yes zone. Again, that is not consent. That is coercion and sexual assault. So remind your children, no matter their gender, that a bunch of 'no's followed by a 'yes' is not consent, and that consent has to be given freely.

What about maybe?

There was an article in *The New Yorker* in 2021 that posited there is no room for 'maybe' in consent conversations. Women, in general, may not know what they want, and therefore, when faced with new sexual experiences, may say no because they don't know. 'Maybe' exists where there is trust – trust to seek consent, trust to stop, and trust to be okay with whatever happens. The idea of 'maybe' is a great argument for taking things slow. But you can only discuss 'maybe' once you know 'no' is respected.

22. How does your phone impact your relationships?

It is obvious to everyone that mobile phones are now part of our lives in a way no other device has been. They are our everything – our point of contact, our social life, our wallet, our reference library, our camera and address book. But what impact are they having on teenagers?

We know that our teenagers are in communication with their friends far more than teenagers ever were in the past. When previously a teenager would spend hours on the phone to a few friends of an afternoon, or in a park with a handful, they now communicate

with hundreds, if not thousands, in group chats or by pushing out their own life events in stories and feeds. But a phone does not replace actual conversation, and texting doesn't replace seeing friends.

The question here is not about what they're doing on their phones so much (although that is an important one to ask), but what aren't they doing. We know (thanks to a lot of research by Dr Jean Twenge) that teenagers aren't working in part-time jobs as much, aren't going out without their parents as much, aren't reading as much and aren't sleeping as much. These activities contribute to a teen's happiness and general wellbeing.

Another thing teens aren't doing as much is having sex. Teenagers, and people in their twenties and thirties, are having sex later, and less frequently. This might make you breathe out a great sigh of relief – less sex means that fear of teen pregnancy becomes more remote, and fears of STIs and slut shaming drift further back in a parent's mind.

The problem with teenagers having less sex is the why. Why are they having less sex? There are, as I mentioned before, a bunch of reasons, and some are fine, or even great (like the fact that young women don't feel they 'have' to have sex with teenage boys, due to the whole 'bad sex' thing, and wanting to focus on university and careers rather than relationships), but there are also a lot of really bad reasons. And these reasons are things you can talk to your teen about without actually sounding like you want them to go off and have sex, because no one actually wants to talk to their teenager about actual sex. So I present to you – how to talk to your teenager about sex without actually talking about sex! Also, the issues here are more relevant to heterosexual teenagers, but there are some interesting issues specifically for LGBTQIA+ teens that I will cover in question 29 (page 220).

One issue we all know about is porn (see question 20, page 160). Porn is a lot more – well, it's a lot, compared to what it was 20 years ago. The average kid sees some form of porn by the time they are 11. Among teens, porn is viewed, for the most part, by boys. There are whole porn industries responding to kinks and fetishes. In 2019 Pornhub's top three searches were amateur, alien, and POV (for Point of View, used in virtual reality ... I'll let you mull that one over). But, more disturbingly, there is some evidence that boys' brains are changing as a result of watching and masturbating to porn. If they can enjoy porn and get off watching it, why bother with the very involved process of actually flirting, texting and dating an actual real-life girl, who is (hopefully) never going to let you do the kind of things you've been watching online?

Porn is also leading to a disconnect between a teen's physical sexual life and their actual (not very sexual) life. This means that there are trends in society (most of this data is from Japan) that refer to 'herbivore boys' who don't actually want to have sex with a physical girl and find the whole process 'tiresome', meaning that sex is entirely solitary. This then leads to a fascinating dilemma where teenage girls, primarily less affected by porn, are actually wanting more sex than their male counterparts.

Another issue is that teenagers, and most people in general, are having less sex because they're scrolling their phones. Not for porn, just scrolling. The use of phones and social media have led to decreasing rates of teenage sex (and alcohol and drug use) because we're all too busy scrolling to get jiggy with it. What has increased, however, are anxiety and depression rates. Sex is a primal need, but somehow we have overridden it by using our phones to release the dopamine hit we get with every ping and notification. And the time spent online is taking away from time spent talking to actual people, which then means any social interaction is really difficult, and causes more anxiety.

So, you have these anxious teens on their phones, scrolling away, not standing outside the local milk bar or cinema having awkward conversations with other teens. Instead, they're talking to each other online, and often in a far more direct and uninhibited way than they would in person. Dating apps have added to this, with many people in their twenties talking about how they download an app to have the conversations, but then are too scared to translate online chats to IRL dating. Instead, they are used for brief hookups rather than starting actual relationships, and we end up in this really messy social situation where young adults are unable to flirt, don't know how to have sex with another person, and are generally lonelier and more anxious than they were at the start of this question.

So, now you know all that, I want to give you some ideas on how to actually correct some of these issues through easy (and not so easy) conversations with your teen.

Edge out time in the day for your teen to do something that doesn't involve their phone – whether it is going for a walk, asking them to pick up some milk, reading as a family, watching the news on TV (rather than on a device), getting some extra work done or doing more chores. All this time when your teen is doing something OTHER than being on their phone contributes to their mental health.

Also, get your teen to ask someone on a date, and make them actually go. Support dating. Support afternoons spent with someone they're crushing on. Have clear boundaries about sex and what the rules are, etc. etc., but if the goal is for your teen to be able to interact with other humans, they're going to have to interact with other humans, and that takes time.

Talk to your teen about hooking up, and about what they do and don't feel comfortable with, but also talk about love. Love is not the point of every hookup, but the point of every interaction can't be just hooking up, either. Otherwise your teen may emerge from their twenties with no idea what love even looks like.

23. How influenced are you by your peers?

Teenagers look to their peers for connection, for validation and, evolutionarily, for survival. There are also functional developmental benefits to teenagers hanging out with each other, according to Professor Abigail Baird, who wrote and narrated an excellent audio series called *Welcome to Your Teenager's Brain*. Time with peers is normal and good. However, the habit of seeking validation from peers can mean teenagers sometimes find themselves doing things they know aren't right, or that aren't aligned to their values, because they'd rather risk messing up than standing out. But what is the difference between the teenager who falls victim to every case of peer pressure and the one who holds firm, rooted in the soles of their feet, and in their souls, to who they are?

We all want our teens to be the latter but, take it from me, after a decade of teaching I can tell you that very few are. And when they are, it is less a breath of fresh air and more like being dumped by a wave, so counter-cultural is it for a teen to be themselves. I have had some students like this, and some teenagers who I haven't taught but have seen grow up. What do they have in common?

They know their own character. You know this because they will willingly admit to their weaknesses in a conversation. Not as a reverse brag, but because they know their strengths and can communicate what they can and cannot do, or who they are and who they are not.

A lot of this comes back to character strengths (see page 85) – understanding what their strengths are naturally, and what they are not. When a teenager knows who they are, if they feel the pull away from their values they know to respond to their internal heebie-jeebies and stop.

The teens I am talking about are not immune to stupid decisions, but they don't define themselves by them, either. They are resilient because they know who they are, and they know they are loved. Their character is not put into question by one or two stupid decisions, because it takes a habit to change who you are; it doesn't happen overnight.

Teens are less likely to succumb to peer pressure when they have people they can turn to about the problems they are facing. Especially in the case of teenage girls, having someone they can talk to who is a 'feisty older woman', as psychologist Steve Biddulph refers to them, gives them a touchpoint for advice from someone who is not their mother. Embrace these kinds of relationships, because they build resilience and strength.

Finally, your teenager is going to make stupid decisions, and you cannot stop them. But raising them with clear values – including, most importantly, the knowledge that they are loved unconditionally – will help them manage when they do.

24. How are you feeling?

Here's what we know – we know that there are increasing rates of anxiety, depression and suicidal ideation in teenagers. There is a lot of data on this; according to Beyond Blue, an Australian mental health organisation, over half of mental health issues we experience will have started by age 14. One in 13 people aged 12–17 will consider a suicide attempt, and one in 40 will suicide. Major depressive disorders are more likely in teenagers (5 per cent) than children (1.1 per cent). Suicide is the leading cause of death for young Australians.

We still don't totally know why. There are some very big pointers to mobile phones and social media being major contributing factors.

Dr Jean Twenge writes in her book *iGen* that one of the biggest issues is not necessarily the use of smart phones, but all the things teenagers aren't doing when they're on their phones – they're not playing outside, not seeing friends, not working, not dating, not really doing a whole lot. And all those things they're not doing are the things that are known to make us happier. In fact, we know that sleep contributes hugely to teenagers' happiness, and sleep is the first thing stolen by phone use.

I have sat through various presentations on teen mental health, and have had conversations with students about it, and it seems to always come down to this:

- Teens need to belong.
- Teens need to find and achieve their purpose.
- Teens need to have some control.

We all need to belong. The evidence for the impact of relationships on teen mental health – on all of our mental health, in fact – is huge. The Harvard longitudinal study mentioned on page 35 consistently shows that positive relationships are the single biggest factor in a person's happiness.

We all need to achieve something, to have a purpose. And purposes change. In fact, as I write this I can feel my purposes changing as my own kids grow older and less kamikaze-like in their risk-taking. I feel pockets of my mental space opening up.

For teens, their purpose is mainly to figure out what their purpose is going to be and who they want to be. This in-betweenness is hard for many teenagers to navigate, and can be a cause of much distress. As a parent, you can be steady in your support without trying to push them down one particular path.

And of course we all want some autonomy, some control. If your teen has been raised with increasing responsibilities, they will have a degree of autonomy. I have often seen the impacts on kids and teens who can't control what's happening around them – family break-ups, friendships changing or friends moving away. They seek control in ways that can be destructive.

All of this is to say, talk to your teen about how they are feeling and invite honesty. Tell them you know how hard it can be, and really listen to how they respond.

As Beyond Blue says, mental health should be about wellness, not illness. Talking to your teen about their mental health and how they are feeling is about keeping them well, not curing an illness. If you think your teen does have mental health issues, talk to your GP.

25. Can you trust your gut to help keep you safe?

This is not so much about physical safety as it is about psychological safety. I touched on this topic in *50 Risks* without really diving into it, because up until the age of 10 the laws around letting your kid go out and do stuff on their own have more shades of grey than an EL James novel. But we do expect teenagers to go out and do stuff. Get to school, go to the shops, hang out with friends, go on dates, sleepovers, parties, trips.

You cannot supervise your teen for these activities – these are part of individuating. You can't even really tell them how to behave or what to do. Well, I mean,

you can – go nuts – but I am certain the response will be 'yeah, yeah'. What you can do, though, is ensure your teen understands what it means to feel safe, and what the absence of safety means too.

The feeling of safety, of trusting your gut, is an instinct we need to develop. As adults, we can all cast our minds back to a time when we did not feel safe, felt awkward, had a weird interaction. As we experience these moments, we start to trust our instincts about them. It is hard to develop that instinct, however, when not given the opportunity or when someone belittles your concerns.

We know what it feels like to be physically unsafe. Like, I haven't met any bears myself, but I have shared my bedroom with some pretty big spiders. Physical safety is something we're all pretty clear on, I think.

But what does being psychologically unsafe feel like? To feel coerced, to feel like someone you're spending time with can't be trusted, or that someone is just not nice. To feel uncomfortable.

Talk to your teen about trusting their gut.

I don't need to tell you how to tell your kid about the heebie-jeebies, because we've all experienced them. Explain to your teen that this feeling is a physical reaction to your brain thinking that you are unsafe, and that they need to learn how to manage it.

When it comes to feeling psychologically unsafe, your teen needs to know they can go to you without any judgement. That you'll come and pick them up if it's that serious, or that they can explain the situation once they're out of it, and talk about what they experienced. Remember, they'll learn more from you listening and being there than they will from you saying 'that was a stupid thing to get yourself into'. They already know it was stupid – their gut told them.

There is also a place here to talk about feeling anxious, rather than about anxiety specifically. We get anxious, that is a normal experience, and stress can be good for you. Kids and teenagers, however, sometimes avoid activities due to that anxiety. As a parent, there is always a balance between pushing your teen to do the thing they don't want to do and respecting their anxiety about a particular activity or place. Make sure they understand that they cannot avoid their way out of anxiety, however. If you are worried about your teen's experience of anxiety, talk to a GP about it.

'If you're slightly other everywhere, you're going to end up being a writer, because there's a part of you that's always outside yourself, observing.'

– LIN-MANUEL MIRANDA

Differences

Teenagers today are different from teenagers of their parents' era, and they see a lot more difference in their lives – in gender and identity, in race and culture, in sexuality, in recognition of privilege. Being a teenager is more of a minefield because the stupid stuff teenagers do is often online for all the world to see, and the risk of being cancelled is huge. Today, there is no space for ignorance, and very little forgiveness.

Teenagers recognise difference more readily and without filter, because everything is new. We see this in children, but it continues through to the teenage (and adult) years. The fewer differences your teenager is exposed to, the more they notice them.

This section is not designed to enforce 'wokeness' on your teen or on your parenting style. It is to help you become aware. Wokeness, for all its good intentions, demands perfection from everyone, and also assumes knowledge that we cannot expect everyone to have.

Experience is the greatest teacher, but not every teenager will experience difference in their own lives, so conversations about it will also help.

One thing I have learned in many years of teaching is this – teenagers may act like they are ignoring you when you talk about your views at the dinner table, but they are sponges and they carry a megaphone when in the classroom. One of the reasons to think about these issues and discuss them with your teenager is not so much to feed a certain bias (although I'm sure some people will say that is what I'm trying to do), but to ensure you are being explicit and clear in what you are saying to your teen about these topics.

26. What's the difference between women and men?

During lockdown, I went down a bit of an Ancient Greece rabbit hole. My kids both became obsessed with Percy Jackson, and I became obsessed with *Natalie Haynes Stands Up for the Classics*.

It is difficult to read Greek myths without getting a tad annoyed at the depiction of women. I mean, really. Ariadne, who basically saves the Athenian princes and princesses from the Minotaur, gets stuck on an island because she's too bossy? Medusa is raped and she's the one who gets cursed for it, not her rapist, Poseidon? And of course Helen of Troy gets passed between kings with zero agency.

But there was something else I noticed down this rabbit hole, and that was that Greek women did stuff. Clytemnestra, before killing her husband,

was running a kingdom. Ditto for Penelope, who managed the island of Ithaca while weaving and unweaving a shroud every day. Women were expected to do things. Farm, hunt and, of course, be intelligent.

Skip forward a few thousand years and Jane Austen depicts a very different idea of what it is to be an ideal woman. Elizabeth Bennett appeared in *Pride and Prejudice* as some precursor to a modern woman – too smart, too brash, and terrible on the piano.

Then came fairytales and Disney movies presenting a very specific type of woman, and along the way the difference between the genders became set, the expectations were defined. It doesn't really matter how feminist you are as a mother, there is no escape from Elsa dresses and princesses. But eventually, every girl has her moment when she realises maybe this is all a load of crap.

For men, the Greek myths tell a very different story. And it is always the same story – of heroism. Odysseus, forced to leave his kingdom because he came up with the stupid idea that if anyone tried to kidnap Helen everyone had to join in the fight. He outthinks and outfights and outmans everyone else. Hercules smashes his 12 tasks. Perseus gets the head of the Gorgon, Medusa.

Male heroes don't change much. They do cool stuff, and they get the girl. Every other male protagonist that teenage boys read or watch is basically a version of James Bond.

What is my point here? Talk to your teen about what they know about the traits of the opposite sex. Because these stories have impacted our understanding of gender today.

For me, a lot of what I have personally experienced is around gender. So it's important to talk about what the actual differences are rather than the expectations of the genders.

A lot of our understanding around difference starts with society and the unconscious biases we have about gender. When my son Jack was born, everyone who saw him used adjectives like strong, wise and alert to describe him. They were active adjectives. When his sister Alice was born, she was cute, chubby and sweet. They were passive adjectives.

Whenever I turn up at an event without my kids the first question I get is, 'Where are your kids?' Usually I scream and say, 'Oh crap, I left them in the car AGAIN.' Their father gets no such question. No father does. It is assumed the kids are with the mum.

There is a gender pay gap, internationally, that has been made worse because of COVID-19, and there is also an alarming statistic in Australia that domestic violence increases by 35 per cent when the female partner outearns the male partner. So as parents,

you get to be angry that your daughter may never be paid the same amount as your son for the same work, but also terrified that she is more likely to be abused physically, psychologically or emotionally if she earns more than her partner.

In Australia in the past year, we have read online petitions of students from well-heeled areas alleging they had been raped at parties. All in the shadow of a political staffer being raped in the Federal Defence Minister's office – and the only person to lose their job over the crime was the victim herself, Brittany Higgins. Just like Medusa was cursed after she was raped by Poseidon, while he remained a god. There are underlying and pervasive attitudes that exist around the safety of women, and these need to be discussed.

Feminism, or 'gender stuff', as some call it, needs to be discussed with our kids, and it needs to be discussed earlier than you think. It needs to be role modelled, because so much of what our teens understand about gender relations comes from home.

27. How can I help you to be a woman who knows her worth?

There are two sides to the conversation about gender. The first is about feminism and how we talk to our daughters about the world. The second is about masculinity and what we are setting up for our sons. All of this is in the context that we do not know as we raise our children who they will be or how they will identify. For me, this goes back to character.

Prior to second-wave feminism, most women stopped working and became housewives when they had kids. That was the done thing. In essence, the part of a woman that wants to succeed or even exist beyond the home was quashed. It just wasn't an option. Thanks to the work of second-wave feminists and women since the 1960s, much has been done to improve the lives of women. But life for women is still not the same as it is for men.

Social and political structures exist that make it harder for women, and that is not going to change overnight, or as a result of a scandal in our parliaments.

The question of 'why don't women do things?' is a question about every single obstacle that stops them. If they are in a co-ed school, they may feel uncomfortable speaking up in class. If they are in a single-sex school, the minute they get to university and sit in a tutorial with the opposite sex and try to talk, they are interrupted or their voices aren't as strong. As one girlfriend said, 'I just shut up for three years.'

Careers are interrupted by childbirth and childcare, and women still carry the vast majority of the mental load at home. The cost of daycare is still mentally (and arithmetically) removed from the mother's (usually part-time) salary. All this keeps pointing to the fact that working through those early years is not worth it.

What does this mean for your teenagers? I can put a no clearer and more pragmatic strategy to you than to 'de-gender' the chores in your household and the way you talk in your home. Reject stereotypes in your family. Dr Judith Locke writes about how boys usually get the 'tougher' but less frequent jobs of cleaning the gutters and taking out the bins, whereas daughters empty the dishwasher and fold laundry, every single day. This means that without even meaning to, without 'putting gender into it', your kids are seeing girls do more chores and boys do less.

Even pocket money isn't immune – according to researcher and author Madonna King, teen daughters in Australia earn around 73 per cent of the pocket money that boys get. And if your son goes to a single-sex school, it probably has far more grounds and equipment than a girls' school, even if they are both public. Donations from alumni to boys' schools far outstrip those made to girls' schools, and parents are more likely to donate to their sons' schools than their daughters'.

None of this is a punishable offence, but it all adds up. It builds a narrative in your daughter's mind that she is secondary to boys, her work is not worth as much, her education is not as important, her value still lies in child rearing.

No one, not even the most conservative of preachers or politicians, wants girls to think they are worth less than boys, but they are treated as though they are.

The issue with 'feminism' and 'feminazis' and 'feminist lesbians' and numerous other terms I have been called online is that it awakens what Professor Carl Jung called the 'animus', or the male in the feminine. Without the 'anima', or the female in the masculine, being awoken too, it looks like women are really fighting for a bit of men's turf, when in fact, it is just very hard to achieve a level playing field.

As parents, we need to actively have the conversation about women and work and feminism, and support our daughters for who they are when society tells them they're expected to be something vastly different.

DEAR ALICE,

From when you started to crawl, you would wrap your pudgy little body around my ankle to stop me leaving – not that I was constantly leaving you, but if I went into another room or left for work. I would dramatically drag you along, saying it was my 'leg workout' for the day.

Women, and people of colour, LGBTQIA+ – actually, almost anyone who doesn't identify as a straight white guy – carries invisible weights not dissimilar to a toddler around each ankle.

These weights represent the added difficulty in daily life. One kilogram comes from knowing that the two greatest factors in being a victim of domestic violence are being a woman and being pregnant. One kilogram is the fact that women earn less than men; one kilogram is women representing only 33.6 per cent of the positions on Australian boards and only 38 per cent of Australian parliamentarians.

The weights are starting to come off. When you finally let go of my leg, it was much easier to walk. I felt stronger and more agile.

Similarly, it is becoming easier for women, thanks to the efforts of those before us, who laid the groundwork and fought for things we now take for granted – the right to vote, access to education, parental leave, no-fault divorce, domestic violence legislation.

Some people will tell you that the weights have been transferred to boys like your brother, Jack. They haven't. They just sit on the ground unused, untouched, and hopefully soon irrelevant. You are able to run much faster without a weight tied to your ankles.

Some will say women getting a look-in through quotas is not based on merit. It may not be, but work hard and your merit will be seen. Some people will call the first women in roles the 'quota hires', but they are more than that. They are the opportunity for little girls to see big girls in positions that once only men sat in. They show you what is possible.

You are still so privileged compared to many. Use your privilege well, and work hard to prove you deserve everything you're given. Be kind, and never be entitled.

LOVE,

MUM

28. How can I help you to be a man of compassion and respect?

When an online petition came out about sexual assault in Sydney's elite schools, I wrote a rant, as I often do, and it was published in *The Sydney Morning Herald*. I awaited mothers of sons with pitchforks and torches who were furious at my suggestion that we need to talk about respect for women at home, and that we need to model respectful relationships.

Author Jess Hill writes in her book *See What You Made Me Do* that there is a 'humiliated fury' in men, because they are set up for failure. Just as in question 27 (page 206) I talked about the daily reminders that our daughters are not as valued as our sons, our sons constantly hear that there is one type of man to be, and if you are not that man, you should be ashamed.

We are killing off the emotional self in boys, what Jung would call their 'anima', and affecting their mental health and relationships. We develop and nurture half their souls. Sport over the arts, construction over daycare, rugby clubs over universities. During the COVID-19 pandemic, the way the Australian government funded 'blue-collar' industries, including sports and construction, showed how the male psyche is taught to develop – switch off the parts of you that do not fit this specific mould and you will have more power, and recognition from those in power.

The problem comes in many forms. Young men who are so filled with entitlement that they expect women to fawn over them and, if they do not, they force them to. Young men who do not fit in in the locker room endure homophobic slurs, regardless of their sexual orientation. So many men I know say they did not fit in at school or uni, and that it wasn't until they were in their twenties that they found people they could be themselves around.

But then, add to the mix generations of girls who have been told they can switch on their 'animus', their male side, by succeeding in sport, in industry, in politics – girls can do anything! The problem with second-wave feminism isn't that it didn't get the job done with women, it's that it didn't get the job done with men.

Testosterone is not a sex hormone so much as it is a status-seeking hormone. Some men need power to give them status, and the easiest way to gain power is to make people around you smaller. This status is not sought in attraction, it is not sought in courtship, it is not even sought early on in relationships. It is sought when some men, who were never introduced to their emotional selves, realise their partners are in one way or another outpacing them. That's when the status-seeking behaviour starts.

This behaviour doesn't just happen with young shacked-up guys. Young men who cannot get laid blame women and feminism for their woes – the involuntary celibates or 'incels' in the worst cases have committed shootings and mass violence, so angry are they at their inability to talk to women, let alone manage to sleep with them. For these men, it is feminism's fault, not theirs. The sex, money and power they believe they were entitled to as part of some vast societal debt was taken not by their own lack of self-awareness, but by feminism. A great example is when the prime minister of Australia said at an International Women's Day event, 'We want to see women rise. But we don't want to see women rise only on the basis of others doing worse.' Who are the others, if not men?

Obviously, this is not 'all men'. Nobody thinks it is. If your first thought when reading this is to get defensive, ask yourself why. And if your view is that boys do not need to change at all, and that society needs to somehow be kinder to them, then thanks for buying this book but let's agree to disagree.

So, what are the pragmatic steps here when talking to teenage sons?

The first is to let them have an emotional side – even if it is just with you or another adult in their life – and nurture it. Do not judge it. Do not call them a 'wuss' or imply that they are in any way 'acting like a girl'.

The second is to role model equality in the home. Even if in your family there is a primary carer and a primary breadwinner, show that both contribute. If you are a single-parent household, make sure they have other adults in their lives who are positive role models as well. Make sure your home has role models of both genders. Kids do better when they have more trusted adults in their lives.

The third is to make it very clear that disrespectful language will not be accepted in your home.

Gender equality has to start with recognising the other in ourselves, and not being ashamed of it.

We need to be aware of the world our teens step into, where not everyone is going to be as 'woke' as you might be. What conversations do we need to have with our teenagers to ensure they can deal with the absolute shitshow society is when it comes to gender?

A lot of people are talking about whether single-sex schools should go co-ed. The reasons are pretty obvious – the world is co-ed, why delay the inevitable? The arguments against are also pretty obvious for heterosexual kids: attending a single-sex school avoids distractions (ahem). But are we overprotecting our teens this way, and not preparing them for the real world, which will not be as kind?

Sadly, there are a heap of stories in the media about a lack of respect for women, so you can use these to start this conversation at the dinner table.

This is not about protecting your teen from every bad thing they could see or hear, but about knowing what they have in their toolkit to respond.

DEAR JACK,

For centuries, especially since white people started exploring and colonising other lands populated by people with different-coloured skin, different languages and different cultures, it has been really, really good to be a white man.

You guys could vote before women. You had universities to yourself in Australia until 1883, and were the only judges on the Supreme Court until 1965. You earn more than women even today, although that gap is slowly closing.

You have been (and arguably still are) in a position of great privilege. That is to say that as a white Anglo-Saxon Australian male, you benefit, and fit very neatly into, the hierarchical systems of Australian society. Watch the news and you'll see that most presenters are still white men. They look like you. So do nearly all the politicians, and businessmen, of course.

It is slowly changing, Jack. Some white men, even ones who claim to be progressive, are angry about that. Yes, these changes mean it will be harder for you to get access to some jobs for a while, as head hunters (the job kind, not the medieval kind) are told they have to hire a woman for a certain job, or someone of colour, or another minority group who has for so long been forced aside so the white men could hold centre stage.

But really, it just means you will have to work as hard as everyone else to prove yourself. And just remember, if there are more opportunities for girls, that means more opportunities for Alice.

You are still so privileged, and should approach every day with an intense and big-hearted gratitude. You will never understand what it is like to NOT see yourself represented in the media, or on TV, or in leadership, and that in and of itself makes you one of the very, very lucky ones.

Use your privilege well, and work hard to prove you deserve everything you're given. Be kind, and never be entitled.

LOVE,

MUM

29. How heteronormative* are you?

There is a unique cruelty to the teenage years. While a proportion of any teen group realises they are not going to fit into a heteronormative expectation, the rest of that group will use their heteronormativity to gain status. Teens seek status, a place on a social ladder, and the easiest way to climb it is to knock people off it.

And being different, being gay, or lesbian, or bi, or queer or trans, or even just not knowing what you are, is a very easy way to get knocked off that ladder.

The teens who at best are a bit uncomfortable around LGBTQIA+ peers, and at worst bully them, are often doing so out of ignorance, or maybe it's

*Why yes, I did do gender studies at university, why do you ask?

because in their own worlds, in their own homes,
it is considered normal to do so.

Certainly it is easier to be LGBTQIA+ now than
it was 20 or 40 years ago. There are LGBTQIA+
writers and role models like Hannah Gadsby,
Jonathan Van Ness, Shannon Molloy and Magda
Szubanski, who have shared their stories about
growing up in a time that Molloy refers to as 'when
gay was a concept that had not been popularised'.
These celebrities are role models for teens who
are experiencing at once a personal and political
process. Because for a lot of LGBTQIA+ people,
the political is personal.

What to say to your teen about LGBTQIA+ people and issues is really very simple. Tell them you love them, tell them that attraction and love can be between anyone, tell them that the kid being bullied is not the only one seeing and being hurt by it. Tell them that if they are being bullied you will fight for them, in their corner, right beside them. Tell them they are loved.

Kids, and teens, also revert to the norm. My kids and I live in Paddington. The Mardi Gras parade travels a stone's throw from our front door, and my kids' closest adult friends other than their grandparents are a lesbian couple, Linda and Kaye. They have known them their whole lives. But still, sometimes the kids look at me quizzically if I say something that may affirm they're in an actual relationship, rather than two friends living together. Teens perpetuate the norm, so normalise difference.

Be careful of your language. Stay informed. The word 'gay' is not used as commonly now to mean 'lame' as it was when I was a teenager. Same-sex marriage is legal in many countries. My father was the prime minister when marriage equality was achieved in Australia. He oversaw the legislation and campaigned for a yes vote in the voluntary postal vote that preceded it. Eighty per cent of Australians chose to vote and 62 per cent voted yes, but I will never forget when my friend Joey said, 'I hate that the guys who put my head in a toilet at school get a say on my right to marry.'

When I checked with Joey that I could quote him for the book, he admitted that now he thinks the plebiscite was the right way to go, because it can never be wound back, as some laws in the US are at risk of being. Once the people said yes, it couldn't be undone.

While stigma around LGBTQIA+ people is decreasing, one study recently showed that suicide rates are two and a half times higher in LGBTQIA+ populations than in non-LGBTQIA+ populations. Especially tragic is the fact that 24 per cent of 12–14 year olds who died by suicide were LGBTQIA+. The problem is that very few families think 12–14 is an appropriate age to talk to their teens about these issues, and about homophobia in general, yet these teens' attitudes can be hugely triggering for other teens struggling with their own sexuality.

But also, hope needs to play a role here. There is hope that it gets better, because it has gotten better and will continue to do so. An optimist can sit in moments of sadness but lives in the hope that better days will come. For young LGBTQIA+ teenagers, the better days are happening, they just aren't surrounded by the right people to share them with.

So please, just love your kids. Even if you are uncomfortable with LGBTQIA+ people for religious or cultural reasons, there is no reason not to love your kid.

30. What do you understand about race?

I originally didn't want to write about racism, so terrified was I that I would be 'whitesplaining' a discrimination I have never felt, when so many others have written far more eloquently on the topic than I possibly could. This is not my place, this is not my area of expertise, this is not my experience. But throughout this book I have written that sometimes we need to have explicit and uncomfortable conversations with our teens. And when it comes to racism, like many other topics, if you don't have the conversation with your teen, you won't know what they know, or where they are getting their information from.

A good friend of mine told me once that he doesn't 'see race, I just see everyone the same'. He can only

do that, and I can only do that, because we are both white, and we have not faced racism.

But racism is everywhere. It is at the most extreme and public levels in hate crimes and genocides, and it is also in everyday life. The Black Lives Matter and Stop Asian Hate movements brought to light for many Australians institutional racism that exists in the US, while also highlighting our own issues with race, specifically with First Nations people and Indigenous deaths in custody.

I do not at any point pretend to understand the struggle of other Australians, especially Indigenous

Australians, who make up just 3.3 per cent of Australia's population but 27 per cent of its prison population. Even more shocking was that during COVID-19 lockdowns in Australia, the notice went out from government health services saying that people over 70 years of age should stay home – that age was lowered to 50 for Aboriginal and Torres Strait Islanders because the risk of COVID-19 is greater for them, a sad reflection of lower life expectancies and access to health services.

So how do you talk to your teenager about race?

You are dealing with four quadrants as a matrix – either you have experienced racism, or you haven't; and either you have acted in a racist way knowingly, or you have acted in a racist way unknowingly. You might at this point say, 'What if I have NEVER done or said anything racist, not even unknowingly?' Either that is very unlikely, or you live in a monoculture. Because, without wanting to deal with any more copyright issues in this book, the song 'Everyone's a Little Bit Racist' from *Avenue Q* may in fact be true.

I think there is one of two conversations that needs to be had. One is for the teenager who may never experience racism, the white kid growing up in a mainly white society. The other is for the teenager who almost certainly has experienced racism in their life, and they may not even have known it as racism. Both involve conversations around self-awareness, and action.

Sometimes, both conversations need to happen within the same family. Two of my good friends are married and living together in the US. The wife is Korean-Australian, and the husband is very much a WASP. More than once, the wife has had to remind her husband that in fact their children are not white, and their experiences growing up are going to be very different from his.

When I was growing up in Australia in the 1990s, racism was pretty clear and easy to see. There were comments about 'Asian drivers', people freely used slurs to refer to Indigenous Australians, and Islamophobia was just starting to heat up. I was buffered from a lot of this for a few reasons. The first is that my parents have always been very progressive and respectful of other cultures. The second is that I took Studies of Religion at school, which meant I had a learnt respect for Aboriginal spiritualities, as well as what I now realise was a pretty basic understanding of Islam (but at the time it seemed incredibly deep). I teach that subject now.

No one says racist things like that anymore, right? Wrong. Sure, we have become more aware of racism as a society, both in Australia and the US. But racism is still there. It has just become more insidious, and more sophisticated. For a person of colour, racism is felt in microaggressions, such as people looking down when they walk past, people not sitting next to them on the bus even though there are no other seats, or being referred to as 'the black' or 'the Asian' friend.

The media is slowly doing part of this job for us. Productions like *Hamilton*, *Crazy Rich Asians* – almost any show produced from 2019 onwards – feature people of different races. The way to see the stark contrast is to watch some *Friends* or

Seinfeld, and see how white those shows were. Representation is important for everyone, but it is especially important for young people of colour to see themselves reflected in the media.

Emmanuel Acho, author of *Uncomfortable Conversations With a Black Man*, talks about racism as having degrees, like crimes do. First-degree racism, such as hate crimes, are like murder. But below that there are lesser levels of involuntary racism, like saying to someone, 'You're not like other black people'. That statement in and of itself is racist.

There are some responses that people will come up with when you talk about race. These kinds of responses will come from people who represent the majority of the population, are generally a bit older, and who will refer to people who talk about racism as 'woke'. I want to outline some of these views so you can talk to your teen about them.

1. Tokenism – people will say adding a non-white person into a TV show, or ensuring there are different races depicted in children's books, is just

tokenism. My response to this is pretty simple –
it is no skin off my nose to do these things, and
it means more than you can possibly imagine
for the people who are now being represented.
But beyond that, it shows that multicultural or
multiracial groupings and settings are normal,
and that is anything but tokenistic.

2. Political correctness 'gone mad' – this is another
   line used by some people I know and, to be
   frank, it drives me up the wall. Societies
   progress and change, and change cannot
   happen without a tension, a friction, a pushing
   forward by the 'woke' kids and a pulling back by
   those who are uncomfortable. This is all part of
   a change that will see our society progress.

3. It is all 'identity politics' – identity politics is
   a problem because it groups people based on
   their identity, and assumes they act and vote
   as a bloc. It's about as fair or intelligent as
   saying all short blond people clearly support
   action on climate change. The thing with the
   identity politics response is that it does two

things. One, it reduces a person to just their identity, and the identity that they are seen as. And two, it can bestow a label ON a person, rather than giving that person the right to choose their own label, or to choose not to use a label. And this is where it gets really messy. So when someone says to or about a person of colour, 'That is just identity politics', that identity could be incredibly important to them, or it might actually have nothing to do with what they are talking about – it might just be something that has been thrown on them to minimise their argument.

The point of this conversation with your teenager is to not let ignorance be an excuse. They need to know what racism is and that it is more complicated than they think. The goal of talking about racism is not to make white kids feel personally guilty, but to make them aware of racism, and of the ways society's infrastructure makes life easier for them and harder for others. Ensure your teenager is experiencing different cultures, at school, as a family, in social groups, on TV.

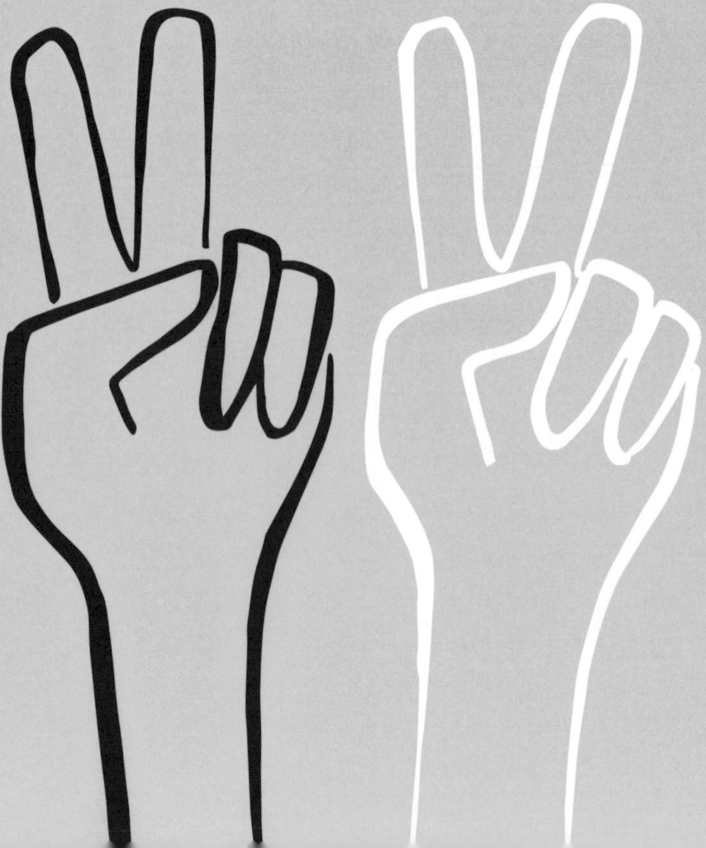

It is just as important to talk to your teenager about racism if they aren't white, because racism can exist in the rejection of self to fit into a white society, to not be as 'other'. And that desire to fit in, and the rejection of self and repression of cultural identity, can have negative effects on mental health down the line.

Regardless of who you are, talk to your teen about racism, because if you don't, who will?

***

I want to thank some friends who have helped me with formulating this question. Maria Wang-Faulkner, who I have known since we were 12, has held a mirror up to my own understanding of race on multiple occasions, which has always made me uncomfortable and I think (I hope) a generally better human as a result. Jordan Shea, an amazing writer and teacher, has provided me with ideas and edits that have again helped me grow. And thank you to anyone else who has had to talk to me about this topic while I percolated and procrastinated on it.

31. What do you know about class?

When teaching Year 7 history recently, I was introducing the topic on Ancient China. Before talking about the social structure in Imperial China, I asked what our society looked like in Australia. Do we have classes? Does anyone have more power than anyone else?

At first, the answers were exactly as you'd expect – no, Australia doesn't have aristocrats like Britain, so there aren't classes. Medicare, the vote, public education – these things are the destroyers of class systems. Sure, cool. Then how come we're in a private school right now? And so the conversation went.

This question is about being clear with your teen about class, and explaining what your view of it is. Class can mean a lot of things to different people. For some, it exists in conspicuous consumption, in real estate. For others, it exists in opportunities, and the opportunities that are available to some but not others. Regardless of your view on class or privilege, it is a concept that will permeate into teenagers' minds, through the media, through aspirational brands, but even in their own lives. Many people find the topic of class uncomfortable, due to either the guilt of recognising their own privilege, or to a sense that they are not where they should be, or where they envisioned themselves.

Talking about class is very uncomfortable, because I know I am privileged. But that does not mean I can ignore the conversation entirely because it is uncomfortable and tied up with some guilt. It is an awareness I have, and an awareness I intend to share with my kids. I already do, in age-appropriate ways. Again, for me, it is in gratitude more than anything.

I think part of this goes to your family's values as well, because teens seek status and identify it in different ways. The size of your home, the car you drive, whether or not both parents work, where you holiday, whether you holiday at all. Teens see class in ways that adults might not. You may be wealthy but put absolutely zero value in the brand of car you drive – or perhaps the opposite is true. Talk to kids about the choices you make and why, to avoid them planting labels on the people they see, and attributing social value when what they are actually seeing is values.

And gratitude: just remember gratitude. Talk to your kids about why they are able to have the thing – because you work, or that it means you can't always be at every school event, but the reward for that is the thing your family enjoys or that your teen ties class and success to. It is important to build gratitude in to balance out any entitlement teens can develop.

And if your teenager can't have the thing, the holiday, the sneakers, explain that it is because that is not an option available to you, or it is an option you do not value, and why.

'Between stimulus and response there is a space. In that space is our power to choose our response. In our response lies our growth and our freedom.'

– VIKTOR FRANKL

Active citizens

We are, as citizens, thrown stimulus after stimulus (not just the economic kind) with little chance to pause and respond. Instead, we either ignore or we react. Ideal active citizenship lies somewhere between apathy and activism. I am not putting down activism. Activism is great, but not everyone can be activists all the time – we need people to go to work and teach and make food and keep society running. And I think making activism the goal of citizenship creates too high a standard, and people disengage.

So, somewhere between apathy and activism, there is active citizenship.

I have tried to avoid the political here, as I do not want to be accused of trying to brainwash a generation of parents and teenagers into believing things like that climate change is real or women shouldn't be killed in their own homes on a weekly basis. That would be horrible, I definitely don't want anyone to accuse me of that.

Some of the questions here are practical, others are 'policy' based, some are just to think about. I hope they help you have conversations with your teenager that lead to more conversations, that help you share your own views, as well as understand the views they are forming.

32. What is around you physically?

This is about a few things, but the most important one is self-awareness. Now, I would love to tell you that this is something teens just magically learn, to give you that sense of relief parents have when nailing potty training during the toddler years – it's okay, not many 18-year-olds are rocking adult nappies. But look around: adults can be just as unaware as teens of their surroundings, especially when there is a device in their hand.

I am guilty of this, and while I'm not excusing my ability to storm down the street furiously listening to Taylor Swift and unintentionally blanking friends and family, I am pretty small and can duck and weave through spaces. I almost lost a date once; I thought I was casually leaving the local markets and he thought I was doing a runner.

But you can still talk to your teen about physical space and help them establish good habits. For example, stay to the left (in Australia or the UK; right in the US). Don't take up the whole footpath. Don't walk wider than in pairs. Notice people with prams, the elderly, those with a disability – and everyone else too, but especially them. Sure, there are places to have a meandering stroll, but a busy footpath is never going to be one of them.

Beware also the impact of crowds. Your teen may be an excellent pedestrian, but you put a bunch of them together and they just. get. dumber. Okay, not dumber, but far less self-aware. And it is far harder to pull their individual training to the fore than it was for Scout to remind Mr Cunningham that he was a good man.

This is not just about walking down the street, though that is very important, and we've all seen people do it badly. This is about self-awareness.

Being aware of where you are, what is around you, what you say out loud (especially in a world of 'overheard in your suburb' Instagram accounts), is a skill that is learned slowly and repetitively. Sadly, it is not one that is easily recognised, but its absence is definitely noticed.

We can develop teenagers' observational skills by promoting mindfulness activities that ask them to identify three things in a room they hadn't noticed before. This is based on the work of Professor Ellen Langer from Harvard University, who sees being observant as a form of mindfulness. It also helps develop self-awareness, as well as other forms of awareness in teenagers.

More specifically, some ways to develop self-awareness in teenagers could include:

AGES 10–13

- Staying on the correct side of the footpath.
- Asking about other people on public transport – is there someone you should vacate your seat for?

- Checking your volume when you speak.
- Picking up litter if you see it.
- Being a good role model to younger siblings (while also remaining a kid).

AGES 13–16

- Avoiding walking in groups of more than two or three.
- Keeping pace with people around you if it is busy.
- Being aware of volume and appropriateness of language.
- Being aware of and giving space to the elderly and parents with young kids.

AGES 16 AND BEYOND

- Parking sensibly – don't waste space!
- Helping those in need when they need it – for example, those with heavy shopping bags, etc. – not all the time, but when you can.

33. What is around you figuratively?

I have a good friend, Daniel, who often reminds me that most people only read the cover of the newspaper, and it's more than likely to be the back cover so they can find out about the sportsball. By contrast, I am a consumer of several news sites, apps and podcasts, because I want to understand what is going on.

Teenagers are in a different position entirely – they get a lot of their information from their peers and online. Psychologist Dr Emily Lovegrove said that while teenagers have always sought knowledge and approval from their peers, the internet has 'amplified and facilitated that instinct to find the peer group they identify with. And it has given them a huge amount more access to much more information, very quickly.' This can mean that your teenager is faced with an onslaught of information before they're even aware of what the point of the news actually is.

The idea of your teenager learning about the news from seeing it on the TV (for example, I can sing the ABC news theme from when I was a kid; does your teenager know it?), or hearing it on the radio in the car, or the paper being left on the kitchen table when you're done reading, it is no longer relevant. It is everywhere.

Getting into the news can be difficult at first. A lot of news stories are built over months, and you need to understand the context to really know what's going on. A great way to manage that is to talk about current affairs as a family. Even if your teen seems very bored by this, it will provide some foundational knowledge. Also, help them identify topics they are passionate about, and discuss issues affecting those topics.

I would suggest that it is healthy to consume the media at a level somewhere between apathy and doomscrolling. On some topics I am fairly apathetic, while others will send me down the rabbit hole. We know that doomscrolling, as it is termed, is bad for us. The amount of time we spend consuming negative news is impacting our mental health, and we are developing anxiety about things that we as individuals cannot control. Loretta Breuning, PhD, argues that 'Our brain is predisposed to go negative, and the news we consume reflects this', which then means we follow the news to be reassured that yes, it is all terrible, and thus we become anxious about how to keep ourselves safe. Breuning argues that we should limit our news consumption to one block a day – like we used to. The sound of the news starting at 7 pm was a daily event in my home when I was growing up.

So while we do want our teens to develop curiosity about the news, and the world around them, we want that to be a healthy curiosity, one that maintains an understanding of our own limitations and does not see us descend into obsessively checking for bad news. I think a lot of this comes from nurturing what they are naturally interested in, and reminding them of what they can, and cannot, control.

At some point it is also good to explain that there is a difference between reporting and opinion. In Australia, that difference can be miniscule, but in other countries it is easier to discern. Opinion pieces are fine – at this point I will declare that I read the Sunday papers each week purely to know what Jacqueline Maley thinks, and am almost always reaffirmed that I am sane in my opinions, so matched are they. But it's important to also read opinion pieces you disagree with, to develop perspective and avoid the echo chamber of a lot of media. It is also important to teach your teen to recognise the difference between fact and opinion, and to recognise the impact opinions have on facts.

If your teenager sees something on social media that outrages them for some reason, try not to dismiss it by saying, 'You don't understand that' or 'Yeah, that's just how it is'. Instead, ask questions that help your teen develop more of an interest in the topic. A naive misunderstood outrage could develop into an active curiosity about the world. And of course, studying history is the answer to many of these problems – source analysis, understanding our world, the constant repetition it brings. Studying history at its heart develops the skills to have a critical knowledge of the media.

34. Where did you hear that?

As I write this, the COVID-19 pandemic is still happening, but hundreds of thousands of people were vaccinated yesterday so I have to have a bit of hope. There have been misinformation campaigns about vaccines through the media, through Facebook groups and other social media. One friend ended up having the phone number for an anti-vaxxer from a poster mistaken for his. Australians seem to be particularly hesitant about getting the COVID-19 vaccine, especially compared to those in the UK and US. A lot of that hesitation is due to the conflicting information that's circulating online. But here is the thing: we need to talk about misinformation and teenagers. Just remember, however, your teenager can disagree with you without being the victim of misinformation.

There are conversations we need to have, and questions we need to ask them:

- Where are they getting their news from?
- How and with whom do they discuss the news?
- How reliable is that source and that person?

I think it is also important to remember that a teen is far more likely to be apathetic than they are to be an activist. However, in my decade of teaching I have seen that change. Maybe, in fact, we do have something to thank Trump for – he pissed off teenagers enough to actually make them think about current affairs.

It is also important to talk to them about the kind of news you consume – is it more progressive or conservative, or do you read both? How does this shape your view? How biased is your news? Can your teen pick bias from an article?

Often people cling to anecdotes over data. Stories are of course important – we remember stories better than data – but anecdotes are often built in falsities and need data to support them. Facebook serves stories. But for every conspiracy theorist on Facebook, there are great journalists and publishers writing news, and creating podcasts and reliable Instagram stories. Guide your teen towards reliable sources that are delivered in relevant ways.

If your teen is apathetic to the world around them, I want to say don't worry, because they'll get there. But one way to help them develop an interest is by integrating current affairs into the daily rituals of life – morning radio or podcasts, having a newspaper delivered (if they are still a thing) or having the news on while making dinner. Discussions about the news at the dinner table are important as well.

Teenagers are easily influenced by the world around them, by advertising and by their peers. We know this. I could throw data at you to prove it, but if you're reading a book about teenagers then you are probably in close proximity to one, and don't need to be convinced on this point. The amount of 'influencing opportunities', however, has increased exponentially since you and I were kids. When I was a kid, it was TV advertising, shop windows and what the cool girls wore on mufti day.

Today, teenagers (and kids, too) are exposed to much more influence, thanks to the volume of advertising on YouTube videos, social media ads and social media accounts. Talk to your teenager about advertising – make them aware of the impact it is having on them. Talk about the creation of needs that are not real, and the role of algorithms in controlling what they see online. Also that there is fact and there is opinion. Alternative facts are not facts – they are false.

35. What is the right thing to do?

A friend of mine, a novelist, talks about how when she is developing a character she will wonder how that character would respond to situations she is in. So, boss dumps a huge amount of work on her desk – how would that character respond? I often think of this when considering my own children and students I have taught. Do I know how they would respond to paperwork at 5 pm, a $50 note on the footpath, or a burglar in their house? What you are doing when you think this way is considering how your teen's character will be in practice.

This question is not designed to tell you what is right and wrong, because I certainly don't know, but

to raise the question about ethics with your teen. Raising the question is the first step in understanding and developing their moral compass. Helpfully, there are heaps of ethical issues flying around all the time. The ethics of climate change, of gender relations, of racism. Should we eat meat? What makes a good person?

The idea is to think about what and how we define right and wrong, good and evil. I don't think we spend enough time considering big ethical questions – but then, I have a masters in theology, so thinking about big, intangible and unanswerable things is what I like to do.

The early teen years are a great time to talk about this. When your teen really gets into superheroes, talk about the ethics of superpowers. How many lives does Batman need to save to be good, and why does he have to save more lives than us? If I saved a little old lady crossing the road, I'm set, right? Heaven, paradise, clean slate, whatever you believe, I'm in. But if Batman ONLY saves one person, then he's lazy?

What about the idea of which lives are worth the most? The COVID-19 pandemic gave us a lot of ethical issues to work through – the ethics of staying away from people we love to protect them, even though that very absence could have long-lasting impacts on their mental health. The ethics of vaccines and who gets one. The ethics of toilet paper – why did so many people bulk buy toilet paper? Were you a good person for not bulk buying toilet paper, or were you only good if you gave toilet paper to a neighbour who needed it? What about the ethics of mask wearing? In Asian countries it is considered a normal thing to do. In America (and Australia), it became an issue of personal freedom for many people.

There are great resources to talk about ethics and the different philosophical perspectives on ethical issues (and I've listed some on page 345) but, honestly, you can start by just asking your teen what they think, and offering different perspectives for them to consider. These conversations don't have to happen all at once, but over time. You might even be surprised by how much they've already thought about this stuff.

36. How can you keep an open mind?

It seems like teenagers, or their parents, are the last people who need to be told about cliques and groupthink. I mean, they spend more time in a high-school playground than we do, and groups are nowhere more visible than there. Groups are formed by people who agree on something, be it music, a favourite sports team, or issues.

When people all share a view they think like a team, and when you think like a team it shuts down any open-mindedness, according to social psychologist and author Jonathan Haidt. This is why the most closed-minded group of people you might know are probably also the most socially progressive and adamant about their open-mindedness. It's one thing to be open-minded as an individual, but it is very hard to agree with everyone in your team while remaining open-minded. This is because open-mindedness requires not only that the mind remains open but also that there be stimulus to keep it that way.

This feeds into identity politics. Because it can be hard to remember or to stick to the actual content the team is connected by, we focus on the people on the other teams rather than the policies. Trump, of course, was the pinnacle of this. He was what people hated, or loved, when in fact the content of his ideas weren't things a traditional Republican would agree with. Team members then justify elections not going their way by attacking the people who didn't support the team, rather than the policies themselves. This shows a collective lack of self-awareness. Marcus Aurelius said that 'your mind will be like its habitual thoughts; for the soul becomes dyed by the colour of its thoughts'.

Open-minded people connect with other open-minded people and, in furious agreement with each other, their team becomes closed-minded. They become an echo chamber. Add social media to the mix and this can get nasty at best and deadly at worst.

Age is also a factor here. The year you were born influences the way you vote. This is because we are all shaped by the big political issues of our teenage years. Amanda Cox in The *New York Times* wrote about how events that occur when you are 18 are three times as influential on your political views as those that occur when you are 40. The teenage brain is more malleable than the adult one. This means people who were teenagers during the Vietnam War continue to be more progressive than those born before or after. I can only imagine how today's teenagers, faced with a climate crisis and the #metoo movement while locked indoors during a pandemic, will vote.

Open-mindedness, or the ability to switch to open-mindedness and what Daniel Kahneman would call 'slow thinking', is important for problem-solving and perspective. In life, you will regularly try to win someone over to your side of an argument – be it what to order for dinner or which political party to support. Minds are changed in the vast space of open-mindedness, in connecting on the issues that matter to a person, rather than by attacking them for being wrong. This can be incredibly difficult, especially when you are discussing an issue that means a lot to you, but that ability to start in the middle, to persuade, can only happen when you can see the other person's perspective and help them understand yours. That takes an open mind. This is where a lot of the questions in this book can help – understanding ourselves, other people's perspectives, focusing on the truth at the heart of an argument and, of course, a never-ending love of history, will all help your teen keep an open mind.

Raise a teenager who has these skills and their values will be clear, but their understanding of others will be far more useful. Because if you want to change someone's mind, you have to be willing to have yours changed too.

'If anyone can show me, and prove to me, that I am wrong in thought or deeds, I will gladly change. I seek the truth, which never hurt anybody.'

– MARCUS AURELIUS

'As long as you
have parents,
you are still a kid.'

— ALICE TURNBULL BROWN, AGE 4

The coaching parent

Every one of the questions in this book could fit into the 'coaching parent' section, because they are all designed for you – the parent, carer, teacher, whatever your role – to shape a conversation around. But the questions in this chapter specifically are about the relationship we have with our teenagers as parents, and dealing with how that relationship changes.

As parents, our goal is to help our kids grow into fully functioning, independent adults. Essentially, parenting involves an utterly emotional, rewarding and draining 18-year handover process to the next person in your role – your child. The parent of a teen especially has this almost impossible task of managing who your teen is right now and who you want them to be at some point, while also trying to actually, I don't know, make dinner or a living and decide if you really care that they sassed you and oh God, do we have to hold everything and everyone to account?

The questions in this section are questions for you to ask yourself, or your co-parent, or your own parents, as well as some you might raise with your teen as a way to explain your view and your wants for them.

We are utterly desirous for our children – we want so much for them. As I typed that I wrote 'too' instead of 'so' – Freud would agree. Maybe we do want too much for our children, and maybe we put too much of that responsibility on our own shoulders. They are, as we have known since day one, their own souls with their own personalities. Can parents really be blamed for everything, as we worry we are? We blame the parents of kids we don't like but shudder to think that anyone would do the same to us.

The coaching parent is not doing the work for the teenager. They are advising from the sidelines. They aren't telling the teenager what to do, they are asking the teenager what they think they can do. They pose questions that make the teenager look within themselves to find the answer, much as Socrates did in the Academy, expecting students to use reason. These questions are designed to start conversations that will go on forever. Enjoy asking them, and relish the responses as your teenager grows.

37. What kind of parent am I?

I think we have all had that moment of being near a parent in a supermarket or a football field and realising that over there is *that parent* and we are very glad to not be *that parent*. It does pose the question though: what kind of parent are we? And how does that impact our teens as they grow up?

I originally titled this 'pulling rank on autonomous teens'. Do you have an autonomous teen? Congratulations! You have a teenager who knows themselves, and who you generally trust not to do the really stupid things. Hopefully, if they are thinking of doing the really stupid things, they might even check with you. Nothing says great parent–teen relationships like the text message, 'Hey, I'm thinking of getting a tattoo of the name of the guy I just saw on the bus, thoughts?'

But hot tip – you are still the parent and you absolutely can still pull rank. You can, and you should. This doesn't have to mean using your teacher voice, but responding in ways that maintain the relationship. This is about the parent you are currently, and also the parent you want to be as your teen approaches adulthood.

One way to do this is what Dr Judith Locke would refer to as 'happy shrugging'. Saying 'I don't care' or 'hmm' does not mean you don't care about your teen, it just means you are not going to indulge their crap. And sometimes, let me tell you, it is total and utter crap. Overresponding feeds the crap-spinning beast. So shrug when they tell you they didn't do the chore. Make them work at explaining themselves, rather than saying, 'Oh, that's okay!'

Authority doesn't always come in booming voices, either. I remember at one parent–teacher evening a slightly frazzled mother said she just couldn't stop her daughter watching Netflix instead of doing her homework. I blurted (because these meetings are the equivalent of speed dating, and there's no time for nuance or subtlety), 'Change the Netflix password.' The mother's response was, 'Really? I can do that?' Remember that as they grow and become autonomous, you are still the tax-paying adult handling the mortgage or rent, utilities and Netflix account in your name, not theirs.

Often in parenting psychology, and in school staffrooms, there will be discussion of the four types of parents – the authoritative, authoritarian, laissez-faire or permissive parent.

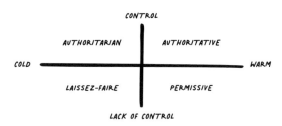

It is a matrix with control and warmth. If you have been an authoritarian parent with high control and low warmth, remember the goal: what do you want your relationship with your teen to be like as they become an adult? That relationship does not come from the amount of control you have over them but from the warmth you show them. While I'm not suggesting you become a totally permissive parent, there is a relationship between the amount of control and the amount of individuation as they become adults. Remember the rubber band we discussed earlier? The tighter it's held, the greater the snapback.

As your relationship with your teen progresses through adulthood, the dynamic moves from being based around control to being based around warmth. Rule-making becomes more about advising, and this is where having some set values can help (see question 8, page 82).

If you are a permissive parent with a lot of warmth but little control, I am not going to suggest adding control, but I do advise having consistency in how you approach trickier problems, by setting boundaries within a generally relaxed approach. Question 18 (page 142), on boundaries, will help you here.

And if you are uninvolved or really authoritarian, consider an increase in warmth – if for no other reason than to ensure your kid visits you in the aged-care home!

38. Why is my teen embarrassed by me?

A friend of mine is the father of a very almost teenage girl. He told me about the time she wanted to get a hot chocolate with him before school, and ducked BELOW the car window on the way there, so no one from school would see her drive past with her dad. Because obviously that would be hideously embarrassing.

He of course had the rational (and slightly rejected) reaction of asking, 'So, you want me to buy you a hot chocolate even though you're too ashamed to be seen with me?' I can only imagine the eyerolls that ensued.

It can be very upsetting when your teenager doesn't want to be seen with you or is embarrassed by you. Or, just hypothetically, when they ask you not to kiss them goodbye anymore at school drop-off when they're only in Year 2. (I'm fine, I'm fine.)

Just because your teen is rejecting you though, doesn't mean you reject them back. There is no ghosting in parenting. You have to be the bigger person, even if they are taller than you (really, I'm fine).

Dr Lisa Damour talks about teenagers, especially teenage girls, doing this and how it can be particularly upsetting for fathers. This is for the obvious and excellent reason that their mothers have actually been teenage girls. They see the process their daughters are going through from the perspective of someone who has been through it and come out fine.

Dads are really important here. When dads don't persevere with their teens, especially their daughters, this can lead to, er, 'daddy issues'. And

let's not pretend that they don't exist for sons as well. I mean, Oedipus is quite the complex.

This is where being a lighthouse parent is so important – there, constant, safe.

At St Catherine's we do surveys on student wellbeing, and this is what they consistently show: the first relationship to take a hit as your teenager individuates is the one with their parents. The second is with their teachers, and, finally, their friends. And then they reconcile in the opposite order – friends, teachers, parents. In other words, you get the worst of your teen for the longest.

So, embrace how utterly embarrassing you are. How unwoke, how cringeworthy, how annoying. Know it is your constant love and support that will ensure they get through it, and that you come out the other side with a good relationship.

And one day, they'll be happy to walk down the street with you, past their peers. They might even buy you a hot chocolate.

39. What has helped in the past?

'GOOD JUDGEMENT COMES FROM EXPERIENCE,
AND A LOT OF THAT COMES FROM BAD JUDGEMENT.'
- WILL ROGERS

As your teen gets older, the problems they face won't always be brand new. There may even be patterns that you can see that they can't. Either way, your teen will be starting to develop the experience to handle some problems.

One of the best questions you can ask someone when they are faced with a problem is 'What has helped you in the past?' or 'What has worked when you've been in a similar situation?' Whether it is dealing with exam stress or friendship issues, whenever I have asked students this, they have always had a pretty good response.

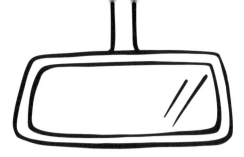

You are actually saying two things here: that you think they've been here before, and that you think they've managed this issue in the past. You are, in fact, reminding them that they can do this.

This is important for teens to hear, because they can get very focused on a problem and not see the bigger picture around it. It is also a great question because, in asking it, you are treating your teen with positive regard, and not just trying to solve the problem for them. You are becoming the coaching parent rather than the didactic one.

The aim of the teenage years is to build experiences so each teen has a toolkit of past bad decisions to help them with future ones. Our knowledge of danger is built on experiences, and we develop those experiences as we grow up. So a teenager who has stacked it on a skateboard will probably have a better understanding of the risks of skating down a set of stairs than one who hasn't. Lived experience is learning, and cannot be bypassed as though it was an iceberg and we a cruise ship.

Now, there will be times when teens still need to be told exactly how to fix a problem, or where your guidance becomes very direct, but giving them the chance to nut it out for themselves teaches them how to, er, nut things out for themselves.

40. Who or what are your influences?

We live in a world of influencers, and that is not going to change anytime soon. The online world basically exists to sell stuff. So let's not even pretend our teens won't be exposed to a great deal of influence.

But it is important to know what and who influences your teen, and whether or not they are even aware that it's happening.

Take YouTube, for example. So much influence happens over YouTube. Kids learn dances and make-up tips and get radicalised on YouTube. The YouTube algorithm is a beast all of its own. Talk to your teen about what they're watching, or even watch it with them. While this might sound painful, it's important to try to get a grasp of what they're watching and learning.

There is something very important to note here – you need to do this non-judgementally. I have written earlier about the importance of naive inquiry. Imagine your teen's favourite YouTuber is like their religion, their beliefs, their worldview, and you said, 'So tell me about this stupid cult that clearly makes money from preying on the uneducated …'. It would not go down well. Instead, ask questions like:

- Whatcha watching?
- What do you like about it?
- What's interesting about it?

If you find it is incredibly mundane, or even dangerous, you can then talk to them about your concerns. You might want to mention how it normalises behaviour you don't agree with, or that you have noticed changes in their behaviour as a result of them watching it.

We cannot escape influence and its effect on us, but we certainly can create awareness about it, and check with our teens about how they are being influenced. This is especially the case with things like porn, but that is another question in and of itself (question 20, page 160).

Influence is an incredibly powerful but also a misunderstood skill. Too little and you yourself can be influenced – we are told to hold onto our own true character as a way to avoid being influenced. Too much influence and you are manipulative. Using our influence is a skill developed in the teen years.

But how do we develop our own ability to influence others, for good? Kids develop this as they grow up: having tantrums when negotiating doesn't work. But in the workplace, in the schoolyard, in your social life, you will need to influence others at some point.

In her book *How to Talk about Climate Change*,
Dr Rebecca Huntley writes about the importance
of teenage girls in influencing their fathers about
the escalating destruction of our planet. 'Teen
girls are the best communicators when it comes
to convincing the unconvinced.'

It is important for teenagers to understand
influence as a concept, because their world is
all about influencers. Those influencers are by
definition influencing others (especially teenagers)
in their inner, hand-held world, so we need to
consider a few facts:

1. Teenagers are easily influenced.
2. Teenagers are often trying to influence others.
3. The ability to influence others is a skill.

We are only influenced by those we see as better
than us, and that means we are constantly
comparing ourselves to others. The saying 'keeping
up with the Joneses' is probably so out of date to
teenagers, yet it's a concept that constantly plays
out in our lives – and theirs.

The Joneses are no longer just our neighbours but every single person on the internet. And while you might hear the arguments or see the actual dirty laundry of the Jones family on their washing line, all you see on *the entire internet* is what they want you to see.

This relates to the psychological idea of 'lakes of comparison'. The lakes of comparison are the groups of people you compare yourself to. When we are young, our lakes of comparison are pretty much muddy puddles, if anything. The kids at daycare might know that a classmate is at a higher reading level, or another runs faster.

As we become teenagers, however, our lakes of comparison widen and deepen greatly to include more and more people. Class sizes go from being 30 to over 100 in a cohort, sport between schools expands, and social events deepen, too.

And then there is the internet. Now I don't want to write a book on cyber safety or responsible use of the internet because that is not my area of expertise (and because it would date very quickly), but there are two key areas to consider.

Firstly, your teen is comparing themselves, in tracksuit pants on the couch, to what is an incredibly curated and selective depiction of someone's life. So the comparison is ridiculous to start with. Don't compare your Sunday night blues to an influencer's filtered and fabulous Friday night.

Secondly, and this goes to a point about friendships in general, you choose what you see online. If a post makes you feel crap, then mute that person or unfollow them. You have control of your socials, and your social life.

But even in the real world, it's worth considering whether comparison can ever be positive. It can. Good, done, next step.

Okay, let's go a bit deeper. Comparison is generally in one of two directions. You are either making an *upward* comparison against someone who is in a better position than you, or you are making a *downward* comparison with someone who is in a worse position than you. It is very hard to compare yourself directly to someone who is exactly where you are, because we are all delicate, unique snowflakes.

Here's a simple analogy. Say your son does not make the sports team. He may focus on Steve, who did, and say it is unfair that Steve is lucky. Instead of buying into helplessness, you can talk about what it actually is that Steve does that got him that spot on the team. Does he train more? Is he just bigger or taller or something? Does he eat better? Two of these things your son can learn and adapt from – more training, more protein. The others he can't, and that's okay too, because there will always be someone taller (in my case, everyone), faster and smarter than you. Get used to it. Focus on what you can control (see question 42, page 294).

But what about downward comparison? What if, instead, your daughter Susie tells you that Rosie failed the exam, OMG, how bad is that?! What do we do with downward comparison? Take it back to gratitude. Not in the #blessed sense, but gratitude for the work Susie did to *not* fail that exam. And also, recognition that Rosie may have difficulties that Susie does not. Awareness and appreciation are virtues to take away from downward comparison – they lead to compassion and service, without pity.

Yes, our lakes of comparison are larger than they were, and far more complex. But comparison does not have to be the thief of joy. It can be the seed of strategy and the font of compassion.

41. One now or two later?

The marshmallow test is a famous psychological experiment in which young children are offered the choice of one marshmallow now or two marshmallows later. The kids who had self-control chose to wait for the double marsh, and some studies have shown that those kids go further in life. In the actual marshmallow tests of our lives, I very rarely pass.

As humans, we are wired to feel anxiety about the immediate future – an exam, a date. But we aren't really meant to feel long-term crises – getting cancer, or climate change. This is why even though we know not wearing sunscreen increases our risk of getting skin cancer, it was such a nice day that we just forgot. Or we know that doing nothing about climate change is going to destroy the earth for future generations, but that's not always at the front of our minds. We are not designed to ponder our future selves at an esoteric level, because otherwise we'd never actually get out of bed, trapped in the fear of not knowing what to take to Aunt Marge's Christmas lunch in three years' time.

Self-control is about prioritising your future self over your present self. Some people find it really easy to connect with their future self. They see where they want to be and are able to envision the steps to get there. When teenagers can see where they want to be, the experience is already happening. These are the students who have their notes updated, or get started on another assessment even though it's not due for a few weeks. They are genuinely hardworking.

I am hardworking, and I have a piano at home. But I have zero connection with a future version of myself that can properly play piano. I enjoy the process of learning, but when I sit down at the piano there is no goal in mind. I don't mind that, because I don't see my future self as a concert pianist.

But what is more often the case is that we DO see ourselves as a future concert pianist, yet we still never sit down at the piano.

That is where the marshmallow test comes in – the need to train ourselves in habits that not only delay marshmallows, but improve self-esteem. For teenagers this is about delaying present pleasures for the sake of their future self. Often this can come as gentle (not nagging) reminders. The work to get to a certain goal often happens before teenagers can see the goal clearly. Doing well in your final exams is far easier when you've worked on writing essays in earlier years.

This brings me to the most cringeworthy part of the book – the marshmallow test is a reason to do vision boards. I hate vision boards, mainly because I'm not very good with scissors, but also because saying my dreams out loud makes me feel embarrassed. However, there is logic to this. Being able to see where you want your future self to be is the first step to practising self-control.

42. What can you control here?

Imagine for a minute you are trapped on a desert island with Margaret Thatcher and someone who is experiencing debilitating anxiety. So you've got one person who said a whole country could pull themselves up 'by their bootstraps' and prided herself on being the daughter of a shopkeeper, and someone who cannot see any way they can fix the situation and feels weighed down by it all.

What you are dealing with here is my overactive imagination, and two very different loci of control. Your locus of control is your 'belief system regarding the causes of your experiences and the factors to which you attribute success or failure'. Someone with an internal locus of control will see success as being due to their own efforts, while someone with an external locus of control will be more focused on (and therefore anxious about) their lack of control.

This is an important concept, because while we want our kids to work hard, and to feel confident that their efforts will translate to success, we also need to avoid arrogance and egomaniacal tendencies. Clearly, 2020 showed us that we are not in complete control of our lives, and sometimes the universe, for want of a better term, throws a lot of muck our way.

For teenagers especially, there is a far greater chance of defaulting to nihilism and anxiety because 'Nothing I do matters, I don't even care, none of it is important' than of becoming Ozymandias saying, 'Look on my works, Ye Mighty and despair!'

An internal locus of control is about being accountable to yourself. That's it. Something didn't go well, maybe you didn't work that hard. Maybe you could have worked smarter. Maybe you just had an off day, but, whatever it was, it was on you more than it was due to the unfairness of the system.

So, how do you have that conversation with your teen?

Firstly, talk about the things we can and cannot control. This conversation could go down one of many potential paths. One will be about controlling people, and question 19 (page 148) will help you there. One will be about the role others have in their own decision-making, in which case go to question 24 (page 186) and discuss the issue of autonomy.

Then talk about why it is good to internalise your locus of control – anxiety is bad, and so is a victim mindset. People with an internal locus of control have far lower rates of anxiety. Plus, someone who can account for their own actions is going to be a responsible and reliable adult. Discuss these points with your teen:

- What could you do? What responsibilities do you have? What are ways you can manage it?
- Focus on (but do not overvalue) what you can control.

As long as we focus on what we can control, the other stuff will just keep trucking. A great example to talk to teens about is the lived experience we all have of the COVID-19 pandemic. There was a lot of anxiety and fear – no one knew what would happen. But those with an internal locus of control understood their personal responsibility – stay home, wear a mask, get tested. Those with an external locus of control still did all those things, but many became obsessed with the things they couldn't control, and their external locus became the foundation of further stress.

Although there are moments in life that we cannot control, when we focus on what we can do, we are ready to respond. We cannot control everything around us, but by owning and being accountable for what we can control, we are better prepared humans.

Kids, and teens, need to learn what they can and cannot control, and that can also involve other people's behaviour. One day, when we were on a holiday with another family, some of the kids were playing bingo. One kid didn't understand the game, so just wanted to watch for the first round. My daughter, Alice, then four, became very upset that they weren't playing 'properly'. In my rationalising with her (practising what you preach is exhausting by the way, don't do it), I said, 'You can't control what other people do.'

To say that made her even more upset was an understatement. But flash forward a full hour, and she was telling all the kids on the beach that they 'can't control what other people do'.

Control is an interesting word. As the national (and global) understanding of domestic violence and coercive control broadens, control is becoming understood as being far more insidious than just wanting things a certain way.

Control is seen in numerous ways with teenagers and, just like their four-year-old counterparts, they are good at managing to get what they want.

There are two sides to this conversation. The first is having firm boundaries around their own controlling behaviour, which they may not even be aware of. The second is talking to them about the behaviour of controlling people and understanding why that behaviour occurs and how to respond to or walk away from it.

The difference between boundaries and being manipulative is control. Some parents reading this now will roll their eyes at the term 'boundaries'. But boundaries are protective factors or signals that alert us to behaviour that pushes them. Boundaries guide your responses to other people (see question 18, page 142); manipulation tries to shape other people.

43. How would you feel about that?

At some point in the past 10 years, I guarantee your teen has said, 'That's not fair!' in an exhausted exhalation. Of course, what they actually meant was, 'That's not in my favour!' You see, kids, and teenagers, aren't naturally great at perspective. Some are amazing, sometimes. Some are pretty good, most of the time. Very few are good at it all the time, although the same can be said for adults, of course.

The ability to see and understand a situation from someone else's perspective is a really important skill. And it is learned. When I'm teaching History and we talk about reliability, to what extent we can 'trust' a source, I always ask students to consider the different perspectives of a wedding. For the bride and groom it's the 'best day of my life'. For the priest it's 'the fourth wedding I've done this week'. For Great Aunt Gertrude, it's a reminder that she should see her family more. Same event, different perspectives.

There are multiple reasons to develop your teenager's ability to do perspective-taking: it develops empathy, sympathy and compassion. It is also important in relationships. Understanding why people act the way they do is part of being kind.

The great news is that this is a really easy exercise. Perspectives are everywhere, and not just in passive aggressively asking, 'And how do you think I feel about that, huh?' Perspectives live in literature and books, and on TV. What are the perspectives of different characters in your teen's favourite show? What about when they have a disagreement with a friend at school? (Note: I wrote 'when', not 'if', because it will happen.) How did that friend see the situation?

As Daniel Kahneman explains in his book *Thinking Fast and Slow*, the thing about considering other people's perspectives is that we have to stop doing something first – we have to stop thinking 'fast': that is, thinking about ourselves. It is very easy to just think automatically about things from our own perspective and assume that is how it must be. But by stopping, and slowing down our thoughts, we make room to think about other perspectives.

So, not every day (because that would be exhausting), and not every time there is a friendship issue, but sometimes, ask your teen how someone else might think about that situation. There are also some great books that explore this. Tom Stoppard's play *Rosencrantz and Guildenstern Are Dead* shows the perspective of two minor characters in the play. Also, Jean Rhys' *Wide Sargasso Sea* beautifully portrays the first Mrs Eyre, who was locked in the attic throughout Charlotte Brontë's gothic romance, *Jane Eyre*. There are characters whose lives, let alone minds, we never consider.

44. What's the worst thing that could happen?

Hi, sorry, not quite done with the whole 'perspective' thing, but you know, 50 is a lot of legs, David, so I'm continuing on. (If you didn't get the *Love Actually* reference, I humbly suggest you suck.)

But here, I am talking about another kind of perspective: putting things into perspective, in fact. In the whole history of the universe, we are but small mites, buzzing around in irrelevance. So really, what's the point?

No, I'm not promoting nihilism, but I am promoting a conscious effort to consider that what may be happening to your teen right now is actually NOT the end of the world. What is in fact happening is that your teen is catastrophising. Now, we all

know that saying 'It's not that big a deal' is about as effective as telling someone who is not calm to 'calm down'. But there is another option.

Professor Martin Seligman, the founder of positive psychology, promotes an exercise known as 'putting it in perspective'. It is incredibly easy and only takes two or three minutes to realise you are being a total drama llama.

Say something terrible happens in your teen's world. Let's say, for example, that they have been asked to see the principal tomorrow morning before school.

Clearly, your teen is about to be expelled, the world is over, and their hopes of being an astronaut have been dashed. According to them, anyway.

So they've actually done the first step already. The first step is to ask **'What is the worst thing that could happen?'**

'I am being called into the principal's office to be expelled.'

'Right, so what will that mean?'

'I'll never go to university, I won't have any friends, I will be destitute on the street. You and Dad will kick me out and disown me, I will in all likelihood become a drug addict and join a bikie gang.'

'Fab, sounds great. **Now what's the BEST thing that could happen?'**

What you might notice here is that your teen's responses will not be nearly as imaginative as they are for the worst-case scenario, because catastrophising is an evolutionary skill we have developed to keep ourselves from being eaten by bears.

'They want to tell me I did well in my English essay.'

'Can't think of anything better?'

'They want to give me a scholarship?'

'So the worst-case scenario is you end up a drug felon and the best-case scenario is I don't have to pay school fees? Come on, you can do better than that!'

'Okay, the best-case scenario is they see I've been working really hard, I get a scholarship, and I'm asked to be the head prefect next year, and am invited to study overseas for university, because I don't even need to finish school because I am that brilliant!'

'Yeah, could be that! **So, what is the MOST likely scenario?**'

'Probably that she wants to meet everyone in Year 12, and it's my turn. Or she wants me to play the trumpet at the ANZAC Day assembly.'

'Okay, **so what is your plan for that scenario?**'

As your teen plans out a scenario in their head, they are actually correcting the brain patterns of catastrophising, and are able to consider plans that are based in reality, rather than their own fears.

So, put it in perspective with them:

1. Consider the worst-case scenario.
2. Consider the best-case scenario (and this will take work, because it is not how our brains work).
3. Consider what the most likely scenario is.
4. Plan for that.

45. Would you talk about your friend like that?

'WHAT ARE YOUR LEGS?'
'SPRINGS. STEEL SPRINGS.'
'WHAT ARE THEY GOING TO DO?'
'HURL ME DOWN THE TRACK.'
'HOW FAST CAN YOU RUN?'
'AS FAST AS A LEOPARD.'
'HOW FAST WILL YOU RUN?'
'AS FAST AS A LEOPARD.'
– GALLIPOLI, 1981

My best friend Melissa is brilliant. She is an outstanding yogini who can twist herself into pretzel shapes, unfold herself and work on business strategy, media plans, or as a TV producer. She is, in short, phenomenal.

I have never had to defend her to anyone, because no one ever talks crap about her. But I absolutely would defend her. And I know what I would say. In fact, I think I know what I would say to defend any friend of mine, because I am very protective of my friends.

Of myself? Not so much. Tell me my outfit looks strange and I will walk around convinced that everyone is looking at me, and not for a good reason. When my boss calls and asks to see me I often respond with 'Am I in trouble?', just so I know what I'm going into.

The point is, we need to protect ourselves and talk about ourselves the way we do our friends. 'You are so smart, you are going to ace that test/interview/ date. They'd be stupid not to hire/fall in love with you!' Sounds like the kind of thing we would breezily text to a friend without a second's thought, but would never say to ourselves.

When talking to ourselves, we fall into the trap of *automatic negative thoughts* (helpfully known as ANTs). In the spirit of brutal honesty, here are mine:

- You suck and people are only interested in you because of your parents.
- You are loud and annoying.
- You don't fit in anywhere.

- You are not smart and you don't know as much about the world as you think you do. (Ironically, I now meta-criticise myself.)

Okay, okay, I know they're not really true. And there is a reason for that. ANTs are irrational, they are based on fear. They are not real. But damn, they're effective when you just want to curl into a puddle on the floor and feel crap about yourself.

Luckily, there is a solution – *performance-enhancing thoughts* are little mantras you can repeat to yourself to correct your ANTs. They are the fluffy white puppy dogs to the scary bullants climbing over your self-confidence. Or maybe they are the anteaters? So here are my PETs:

- You are a kind person with wonderful friends.
- People who suck don't get book deals.
- You are loud, but you are also listened to.
- You are smart, and a lot of your intelligence is intuitive.
- You are loved, and loving.

I think we can all agree that to say the above statements to ourselves would make us feel like an absolute wanker, correct? Good, glad we're all on the same page. Instead, imagine you are writing them about your best friend – it becomes far easier.

The reason for this is that what we say about ourselves becomes a self-fulfilling prophecy. Self-doubt (your ANTs) is based on irrational fear, but the more we say it about ourselves the more real it becomes. PETs can seem incredibly cringeworthy and put on, but they can disarm your ANTs – they are in fact ANTRID.

Talk to your teenager about the way they talk about themselves. Be honest about what your ANTs are and what PETs you might be using to push them back. And then encourage your teen to consider their own ANTs and PETs. And one more thing: make sure none of the PETs are based on looks, marks at school (because they can change) or 'coolness'. Make sure they are innate to who your child is.

Are you ready, Leopard?

46. What do you know about your brain?

We often think of the changes teenagers go through as primarily physical, driven by hormones: boys' voices breaking, girls growing breasts, hair where there wasn't hair before. Hormones play a role in mood too, as any adult will know from their own experiences. But as I touched on in the introduction, a lot of teenagers' more extreme and, at times, seemingly inexplicable behaviour is actually due to their brain function. This is particularly true when they are upset. Helping your teen understand the brain chemistry that drives a lot of their emotional responses can be incredibly empowering, and can help them both manage and understand their feelings.

There is a very neat visualisation by Lindsay Braman, a counsellor and amazing illustrator, of how the brain works when we are upset, which I want to describe.

When looking at your hand and wrist, imagine your wrist is the brain stem that sends messages to your body, like drink water, don't forget to breathe, etc.

If you place your thumb onto your palm, that is like the amygdala. The amygdala is a bit like your security dog. It tells you when you are in trouble, it senses danger, and it is the button to start fight, flight or freeze responses in case of danger. Really useful in the wild, when there are bears.

When you fold your fingers over your thumb into a fist, they are a bit like the prefrontal cortex. This helps us manage difficult emotions, as well as stay calm. But if you try now, you will notice it is very difficult to keep your fingers over your thumb when your thumb starts wriggling around and tries to escape.

That is essentially what happens when we get upset. Our amygdala goes into overdrive. Because a teenager's prefrontal cortex isn't yet developed, it can't yet use higher-order functioning to say, 'It's not a bear, someone just hasn't texted back yet', and they get set off.

So that is why teenagers are emotional: their brain isn't fully developed. That doesn't excuse bad behaviour or mean that you cannot reason with teens when they are upset, but it does explain what is happening.

Now, there is one thing that can help someone who has had their amygdala set off. How it is done depends on your teen, but it is about increasing the vagal tone (connected to the vagus nerve in your brain) to make people happier. There are different ways to do this, such as exercise and singing, but connection with other people is also one. So when you see that your teen is stressing out and their amygdala is in overdrive, the best thing you can do is tell them that you love them, you are here for them and, if they let you, give them a hug. The freak-out is not a teaching moment, but the time afterwards, when they're calm, certainly can be.

47. Who or what are you grateful for?

I am in two hearts about writing about the benefits of gratitude because there is so much on gratitude around these days, and I don't feel I can add any more to the conversation, except to say that in this time of gratitude emojis and 'tag someone who made your day better' posts on social media, a thank-you letter is still an incredibly rare thing. There is nothing wrong with posts or emojis, but to raise a teen who becomes an adult who remembers to write thank-you letters – be they short, or long, with inside jokes or just appreciation, is to raise someone far more aware of the gifts life has to offer.

People who regularly practise gratitude are healthier and happier. Gratitude also makes you more empathetic, which in turn helps you become more compassionate and self-compassionate, which boosts your own self-worth. Furthermore, people who are grateful are more optimistic and aware of the importance of relationships.

Emperor Marcus Aurelius, writing in the 2nd century CE, said one of the things we require in life is 'an attitude of gratitude in the present moment for anything that comes your way.' Sucks to be that influencer who thought they had coined 'attitude of gratitude', huh?

In a world where expectation and entitlement are rife, gratitude means appreciating what we have. Gratitude can be the salve to so many natural assertions in our society – judgement, entitlement, self-absorption. It is the antidote to an overinflated ego, because we need other people; other people enrich us. In *50 Risks* I snuck gratitude in as a risk, not in and of itself but because entitlement is clearly a risk for kids and teens. Focusing on what we already have can shift perspective, and avoid the spiral of ranting we can so easily fall into.

Now, obviously, a thank-you note is not the only way to practise gratitude, but it is a very clear way to do so, and a habit that will be appreciated by any recipient.

So how do you teach a teen to write a thank-you note? Well, start with people close to them. Your teen might think writing a letter is lame, but at least it will be lame in front of people they can be themselves around.

Role-model it by writing thank-you letters, or creating a ritual around writing a thank-you card or letter to someone each week – someone who helped you or hosted you or you are just grateful for, thanks to a friend for a fun afternoon.

A thank-you letter is incredibly easy to write and does not need to be an essay. There are whole websites dedicated to how to write a thank-you letter, but I think the general anatomy of a thank-you letter should include:

- The date, obviously.
- Correctly addressing the person – Dear first name for a friend, or Mr/Mrs/Ms/Dr/Prof and surname.
- Start with a general thank you for whatever it is.
- A reason it is appreciated (even if it isn't).
- Something about the experience or the relationship.
- A message of hope.
- Sign off.

15 August 2021

DEAR READER,

Thank you for purchasing and reading *50 Questions To Ask Your Teens*. I am especially thankful that people read what I write when I have not yet navigated my own children through the teenage years. I can only hope that they will grow up in a world with more empathy, kindness, and understanding of their own autonomy and responsibility, as I hope your children will too.

Kindest regards,

DAISY TURNBULL

Now, I have one girlfriend, Kumi, who adds small origami cranes to her letters, which is beautiful, and incredibly her. There are many ways you can make your own thank-you notes unique, and with a lot of internet-based printing providers, having cards printed can be cheaper than buying them at the newsagency. Please, no glitter, though, it is craft herpes – it never goes away.

48. Which rituals are important to you?

There is something beautiful in rituals. A lot of positive psychology research has reaffirmed that millennia-old traditions had it right – weekly rituals are the way to go. For example, weekly gratitude has been shown to be more effective than daily practices, which can become robotic and rote.

Rituals are important chances to connect with your teen. In *50 Risks* I talked about starting the way you want to go on. Want a kid who likes hiking? Get them hiking. But even if your kid or your family didn't have set rituals before they became teenagers, they can and should be built.

Rituals provide consistency. As a single parent, I have a ritual with the kids where we play rumbles before they go to their dad's. It is really just an excuse for a lot of hugs. It may not last when they're taller than me (so, by the time this book is published) but, for now, it is wonderful. I also have a ritual of tidying their rooms and switching lights off and shutting their bedroom doors after they go. Rituals are protective. They are a form of self-care.

Consistency is important for kids, as it develops their confidence and sense of belonging within a family. Even meals can and should be rituals. Studies have shown that teenagers with mental health complaints ate with their parents less frequently than the rest of those surveyed.

Evidence has shown that sharing meals can help a family develop their identity and model positive behavioural patterns. For teenagers, it helps develop their own identity in the context of the family. Many rituals have their basis in religion. For example, the weekly Shabbat dinner as practised by Jewish families is the perfect example of a family

ritual that also develops individual identity, and of how teenagers change and adapt the rituals of their childhoods to their new adult lives and their own families.

Author Sasha Sagan has written extensively about the importance of rituals in her own secular childhood, and the importance of patterns in creating consistency in our lives.

Modern life may not allow for sharing one meal a day, let alone three together every day. However, COVID-19 certainly did. And across the world, families talked about the benefits of sharing meals together, if for no other reason than to break up the monotony of the day.

But creating a weekly ritual is something that can continue beyond the teenage years. My parents, who are amazing, have Jack and Alice once a week, and we share a meal as a family every week. It is always the highlight of my week. The comfort of home. The kids may one day prefer seeing friends or playing video games, but the ritual will always be there.

49. How do you grieve?

Grief, the mourning for something lost, happens every day. We grieve lost friends and relatives in death, we grieve lost relationships, we grieve rejection, we grieve lost opportunities. We can grieve the smallest of disappointments, and the greatest of losses.

Grief is a part of our lives we cannot and should not escape, and one we cannot really prepare for.

Grief (as all pain) is relative. Your teen may grieve the loss of a friend moving to another school or city as deeply and rawly as you will grieve the death of a beloved uncle who to them is not worthy of a single tear. There are many great books about grief I can point you to, and I have listed these in the resources section (see page 347). But what I have learned, through my own grief and the grief of others, is that it is different for everyone.

Author Glennon Doyle writes in her book *Untamed* that it took until she was a grown-up to realise that 'all feelings are for feeling, even the hard ones'. Grief must be processed. You must sit with sadness, you cannot Marie Kondo it or keep yourself so busy you never have to face it. Like a sodden towel or sports sock in the corner of a bedroom, it will fester if you ignore it.

It is hard to process grief, because at its heart is the fact that we are somehow less ourselves.

I came to Bronte Beach in Sydney to write this because, for no other reason than twee-ness, I wanted to be near crashing waves when writing that grief comes in waves. We know this, we all know this. You can be totally fine and then, like some emotional dumper brought on by a coffee cup or a place or a memory, you find yourself sitting in that exact moment in time when the loss occurred. It is a painful tardis.

Previously I might have written that grief, especially grief associated with death, is not something we experience well in Western cultures; we do not give it the space it deserves. But in 2020 and 2021 we did. We grieved cancelled plans, our worlds becoming smaller, and the ever ticking number of deaths from COVID-19. For us in Australia this was generally abstract, but for those in the rest of the world, it was the loss of relatives, friends, teachers, neighbours.

My good friend Shentel lost her father-in-law during the COVID-19 pandemic, not due to COVID but to old age. Their mourning lasted months, and still continues, from daily services to burning ghost money to venerate their lost patriarch. The Buddhist grieving process is one that gives you no other option but to travel through and out.

What do Anglo-Saxon rituals give us? Half a day off work if they were a close relative, a funeral, drinks after. Anglo-Saxon mourning is confined to a finite amount of space and time, and continued grief is rarely accepted.

Even the process of Swedish death cleaning pre-empts grief, trying to remove the pain and time of your loved ones having to go through your things by doing it for them before you die.

Another thing that helps me understand grief is to understand the circles of grief. At the centre, there is the closest griever – the widowed, the abandoned, the orphaned. Then, in each outer ring are people one step removed. The rule is very simple – love in, shit out. From inner circles to outer, they can rant and scream, cry and moan to those around them. But from the outer to the inner rings, there can only be love. Be there, check in, give hugs and tell them they will get through this. Grief gets messy because sometimes those in an outer ring dump back into an inner ring, and that is like an insinkerator going in reverse: it creates mess and conflict.

Note: the circles of grief do not excuse bad behaviour or an abdication of responsibility beyond what is acceptable in your family. But to tell a grieving person, or a grieving-adjacent person, that they deserve love from those around them but can dump their sadness on you, provides a model for getting through without having to isolate themselves.

Another element of grief is the guilt we start to feel when we catch ourselves not grieving – smiling or laughing and then stopping in the inescapable moment of being through the rapids of guilt and in calm waters again.

You can grieve and still laugh. You can mourn and be excited about something. You can hold two emotions at once.

Grief is part of life but, as with many things these days, we try to bypass talking to kids and teens about it, trapped by our own incapacity to process it. I hope these ways of talking and explaining grief help not only your teen, but you as well.

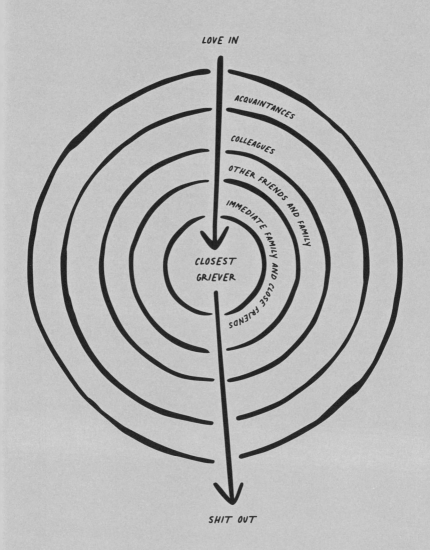

50. What questions do you want me to ask you?

At this point, you have asked your teenager so many questions – these 49, plus, of course, eleventy billion versions of 'Where are your shoes?' But the time comes, as parents, to ask your adult children what *they* want to be asked. What role do they want you to play in their lives, and what kind of adult relationship do you both want to have?

Reaching a certain age does not make us an adult. It is the accumulation of experience and relationships that makes us an adult. In the introduction (page 8) I talked about secure

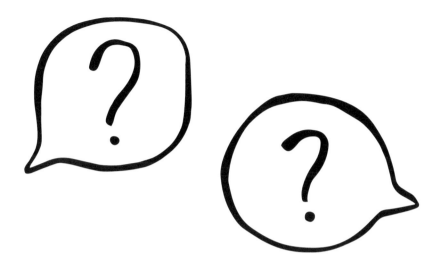

attachment and how important it is for young children to have secure relationships with their parents, based greatly on the concept of 'serve and return'. Secure attachments lead to healthy self-ideation and development of relationships.

But one day your child, who as a baby so lovingly stared into your eyes as you fed them or bathed them, will look at you differently, and you will look back at them with this fear, much like the night after an exam – have I done enough? Did I forget to talk about this topic, or that topic? You did, but it's okay.

Your newly minted adult may also not want to be the adult yet – yes, adulting is hard, but it is the autonomy and the responsibility that they have always wanted, and you as a parent are still there, just differently.

As parents, for as long as you live you will have more years of experience than your kids. But there will come a point where their experiences will not be the same as yours, and therefore, your kids, as adults, will, in their own lives, be more experienced than you.

My mother is my greatest champion, but she does sometimes look at how I am doing life and think I'm a bit nuts (okay, she hasn't said this, but I reckon she does). Two kids, single mum, full-time job, writing in the cracks of time between everything else, busy social life, and crochet. No mother and daughter will have the same experience, even if they are doing the same thing women have done since the dawn of time, because the world changes. I remember when I was breastfeeding Jack and reading the news on my phone. Mum told me when she was breastfeeding my brother there were only broadsheet newspapers to read, so if you wanted to read and feed, you had to have the newspaper set up on the kitchen table open at the pages you wanted.

So your teen will be differently, and potentially more, experienced than you, and there will be generational differences – and that's before you even consider your adult kid's family having different cultures, values and rituals.

As your teen becomes an adult, you need to embrace these differences and be a part of their lives as much as they are a part of yours. Glennon Doyle said a woman becomes a responsible adult 'when she begins to build her island not to [her parents'] specifications, but to hers'.

In recognising that there are now two distinct islands – yours as parents, and your adult kid's as their own, you can respect and coexist in both. At Mum and Dad's place, they set the table in a certain way; I do it differently. I do it one way at theirs and another at mine. Still love them.

And don't worry, they will need a lot from you, at the most inconvenient of times (sorry, Mum and Dad).

On nights when my kids are with their father, I often wake up and run to their rooms, only to be reminded that their empty beds are thus because they are not here. I wonder if I will be able to sleep when they are out with friends in their teenage years. When will the worrying of parenting end?

A few months ago I spent the night at my parents' place with my kids, as we often do, so I could attend my best friend's birthday dinner after my kids finished theirs. I returned at around 11 pm, with the muscle memory of removing my shoes as I came in the front door so as not to wake anyone, sneaking past my parents' room, veering to the right to avoid that floorboard, and climbing into bed with Alice purring lightly in the bed I slept in throughout my teenage years (she is now adamant it's 'hers'). As I was falling asleep, I heard my mum come in to check on me. It will never end, and that is parenting.

Resources/endnotes

INTRODUCTION

The risks of social isolation are real; the loneliness of social isolation can lead to mental-health issues, such as depression. Denworth, Lydia, 'What happens when kids don't see their peers for months', *The Atlantic*, 25 June 2020

Other research has shown that much of this social anxiety has stemmed from not having access to the opportunities ... Volkin, Samuel, 'The impact of the COVID-19 pandemic on adolescents', Johns Hopkins University, 11 May 2020

Psychologist Dr Judith Locke suggests this technique when listening to a rant ... Locke, Judith, *The Bonsai Child*, Judith Locke (2015)

Dr Steve Biddulph refers to them as 'feisty older women'. Biddulph, Steve, *Raising Girls in the Twenty-first Century*, Simon & Schuster (2019)

Harvard psychologist Professor William Pollack talks about the benefits of young men having an 'extra dose of Dad' ... Anderson, Porter, 'All our fathers: William Pollack's "Real Boys"', CNN.com, 20 June 1999

In 1880 in New South Wales, for example, children aged seven to 14 had to attend school for at least 70 days every six months ... Campbell, Craig and Proctor, Helen, *A History of Australian Schooling*, Allen & Unwin (2014)

For example, gangs formed around Sydney between 'bodgies' and 'widgies' ... Moore, Dr Keith, 'Bodgies, widgies and moral panic in Australia 1955–1959', Queensland University of Technology, 29 October 2004

Dr Dan Siegel, MD and founder of the Mindsight Institute, has conducted extensive research on the adolescent brain. Siegel, Daniel J, *Brainstorm: The power and purpose of the teenage brain*, Tarcher/Putnam US (2015)

In 50 Risks I introduced Erik Erikson's first four stages of life ... Erikson, Erik, *Identity and the Life Cycle*, WW Norton & Company (1980)

The biggest factor in life satisfaction is relationships, according to the Harvard Study of Adult Development ... Mineo, Liz, 'Good genes are nice, but joy is better', *The Harvard Gazette*, 11 April 2017

SECTION 1: LIFE SKILLS

As Eve Rodsky describes in her book Fair Play ... Rodsky, Eve, *Fair Play: A game-changing solution for when you have too much to do (and more life to live)*, Penguin Putnam Inc (2021)

If you have read 50 Risks, *you'll know I go a bit fangirly for Richard Ryan and Edward Deci, who created self-determination theory.* Center for Self-determination Theory, 'Overview', selfdeterminationtheory.org/theory

Professor Lea Waters, author of The Strength Switch, *argues that the strengths your teen may have in one arena ...* Waters, Lea, *The Strength Switch: How the new science of strength-based parenting helps your child and teen to flourish*, Random House Australia (2017)

In her book Sacred Rest, *Dr Saundra Dalton-Smith talks about the seven types of rest people need.* Dalton-Smith, Saundra, *Sacred Rest: Recover your life, renew your energy, restore your sanity*, Little Brown (2019)

Dr Lisa Damour has written about the importance of a restorative practice. Damour, Lisa, 'Why teens need a break this summer', *The New York Times*, 1 June 2021

What do you know about money? Pape, Scott, *The Barefoot Investor*, John Wiley & Sons Australia (2020)

Research shows that most kids in middle-class families in Australia are the richest they will ever be BEFORE they finish school. Huang, Yangtao, 'Intergenerational economic mobility in contemporary Australia: Is Australia still the land of the "fair go"?', University of Queensland, 2017

In fact, research tells me that when I was a teenager, I had an extra 100 minutes ... Twenge, Jean, *iGen: Why today's super-connected kids are growing up less rebellious, more tolerant, less happy – and completely unprepared for adulthood – and what that means for the rest of us*, Atria Books (2018)

SECTION 2: CHARACTER

Prior to Christianity, Stoic philosopher Seneca wrote that people should 'Cherish some man of high character ... Seneca, Lucius Annaeus, *Letters from a Stoic*, Penguin Classics (2014)

... the VIA (Values in Action) Character Strength Survey ... Character strength illustrations based on illustrations at www.viacharacter.org © 2004–2021, VIA Institute on Character. All rights reserved. Used with permission.

... proponents of character-based psychology like Professor Angela Duckworth argue that ... Duckworth, Angela, *Grit: The power of passion and perseverance*, Random House UK (2017)

Alfred Adler, a psychologist writing at the same time as Freud, said ... Kishimi, Ichiro and Koga, Fumitake, *The Courage to be Disliked*, Allen & Unwin (2017)

Not to be outdone, Professors Martin Seligman and Chris Peterson came up with the VIA (Values in Action) Character Strength Survey ... VIA Institute on Character, 'The 24 Character Strengths', viacharacter.org/character-strengths

Psychologist Milton Rokeach created a value rating system that he named after himself ... Rokeach, Milton, *Understanding Human Values*, Free PR (2000)

I remember sharing Sheryl Sandberg's line of 'done is better than perfect' ... Sandberg, Sheryl, *Lean In: Women, work, and the will to lead*, Random House UK (2015)

The song 'Hate Dah' By Super Silly has the line 'I roll my eyes when you text my phone ...' Super Silly, 'Hate Dah', Long Mile Road EP, Super Silly, 2019, track 2

In his book Indistractable *Nir Eyal argues that what we actually need to look at is* ... Eyal, Nir, *Indistractable: How to control your attention and choose your life*, Bloomsbury (2020)

Angela Duckworth, who I absolutely idolise, wrote the book Grit ... Duckworth, Angela, *Grit: The power of passion and perseverance*, Random House UK (2017)

A Washington State University study in 2019 showed that in response to the statement 'I am often bored' ... Weybright, Scott, 'Looking at how the brain reacts to boredom could help people cope', *WSU Insider*, Washington State University, 8 July 2019

... when we throw phones at our kids, 'we steal their boredom from them'. Doyle, Glennon, *Untamed*, Penguin Putnam Inc (2020)

... 'when it comes to dealing with painful emotions, the only way out is through'. Damour, Lisa, 'Helping teens make room for uncomfortable emotions', *The New York Times*, 21 April 2020

What brings you joy? Kennelly, Stacey, '10 steps to savoring the good things in life', *Greater Good Magazine*, 23 July 2012

... 'On the internet, nobody knows you're a dog'. Cavna, Michael, '"Nobody knows you're a dog": As iconic internet cartoon turns 20, creator Peter Steiner knows the joke rings as relevant as ever', *Washington Post*, 31 July 2013

Aristotle once referred to the play Oedipus Rex *as having unity of place because it existed in a liminal space.* Natalie Haynes Stands Up for the Classics, 'Clytemnestra', Series 7, Episode 4, BBC UK, 8 June 2021

SECTION 3: RELATING

We know that relationships are the single biggest factor in a person's happiness ... Mineo, Liz, 'Good genes are nice, but joy is better', *The Harvard Gazette*, 11 April 2017

In his book Resilient, *Rick Hanson talks about the importance of understanding the mood we are in and why.* Hanson, Rick, *Resilient: How to grow an unshakable core of calm, strength, and happiness*, Harmony (2018)

As much as I would like to credit her with this idea, it was coined by the psychologist Shirley Glass. Glass, Shirley, shirleyglass.com/introduction

... *'patterns of abusive behaviour designed to exercise domination and control over the other party in a relationship'.* NSW Government, 'Coercive control: Discussion paper', October 2020

Jess Hill, in her book See What You Made Me Do ... Hill, Jess, *See What You Made Me Do*, Black Inc (2019)

Porn is everywhere online and your teenager has very very likely seen it, as most kids have by the age of 11. McKee, Alan, 'Yes, your child will be exposed to online porn. But don't panic – here's what to do instead', *The Conversation*, 17 November 2020

But even more, in an Atlantic *article in 2018 on the teenage sex recession* ... Julian, Kate, 'Why are young people having so little sex?', *The Atlantic*, December 2018

But furthermore, as Dr Lisa Damour discusses in her podcast, Ask Lisa, *your teen creates a link* ... Damour, Lisa, *Ask Lisa*: The psychology of parenting, 'My kid looked at porn. What should I do?', Episode 31, 16 March 2021

... *if you want more information specifically on LGBTQIA+ teen areas, check the resources section.* Minus 18, minus18.org.au; Wear It Purple, wearitpurple.org

Brent Sanders, an ex-police officer and expert on workplace harassment and sex crimes ... Brent Sanders Consulting, 'Creating power through knowledge', brentsandersconsulting.com.au

One of the most concerning things about the 'field theory' ... Zhou, Naaman and Boseley, Matilda, 'Milkshake consent video earlier script referred to "modern progressive" 1950s', *The Guardian*, 23 April 2021

There was an article in The New Yorker *in 2021 that posited that there is no room for 'maybe'* ... Suk Gersen, Jeannie, 'The politics of bad sex', *The New Yorker*, 31 March 2021

Dr Jean Twenge writes in her book iGen *that one of the biggest issues is not* ... Twenge, Jean, *iGen: Why today's super-connected kids are growing up less rebellious, more tolerant, less happy – and completely unprepared for adulthood – and what that means for the rest of us*, Atria Books (2018)

In 2019, Pornhub's top three searches were amateur, alien, and POV ... Pornhub, 'The 2019 year in review', 11 December 2019

... *Professor Abigail Baird, who wrote and narrated an excellent audio series on* Audible *called* Welcome to Your Teenager's Brain. Baird, Abigail, *Welcome to Your Teenager's Brain*, Audible (2021)

... *a 'feisty older woman', as psychologist Steve Biddulph refers to them* ... Biddulph, Steve, *Raising Girls in the Twenty-first Century*, Simon & Schuster (2019)

There is a lot of data on this, but for consistency I am going to use data
   from Beyond Blue ... Beyond Blue, 'Statistics', beyondblue.org.au/
   media/statistics

Dr Jean Twenge writes in her book iGen ... Twenge, Jean, *iGen: Why today's
   super-connected kids are growing up less rebellious, more tolerant, less
   happy – and completely unprepared for adulthood – and what that means
   for the rest of us*, Atria Books (2018)

The Harvard longitudinal study consistently shows that ... Mineo, Liz, 'Good
   genes are nice, but joy is better', *The Harvard Gazette*, 11 April 2017

SECTION 4: DIFFERENCES

... alarming statistic in Australia that domestic violence increases by 35 per
   cent when the female partner outearns the male partner. Wright, Shane,
   'When women earn more than their male partners, domestic violence
   risk goes up 35 per cent', *The Sydney Morning Herald*, 30 March 2021

Dr Judith Locke writes how boys usually get the 'tougher' but less frequent
   jobs ... Locke, Judith, *The Bonsai Child*, Judith Locke (2015)

Even pocket money isn't immune – according to researcher and author
   Madonna King ... King, Madonna, 'What our kids' pocket money says
   about the pay gap', *The Sydney Morning Herald*, 4 July 2018

... awakens what Professor Carl Jung called the 'animus', or the male in the
   feminine. Leser, David, *Women, Men and the Whole Damn Thing*, Allen
   & Unwin (2019)

... women and representing only 33.6 per cent of the positions on boards ...
   Australian Institute of Company Directors, 'Board diversity statistics',
   9 June 2021

... and only 38 per cent of parliamentarians. Issa, Antoun, 'Gender breakdown
   in parliament: Australia beats UK, US, Canada in female representation',
   The Guardian, 31 March 2021

Author Jess Hill writes in her book See What You Made Me Do that there is
   a 'humiliated fury' ... Hill, Jess, *See What You Made Me Do*, Black Inc (2019)

Testosterone is not a sex hormone so much as it is a status-seeking hormone.
   Harmon, Katherine, 'Testosterone bumps up status-seeking behavior, not
   aggressive risk-taking', *Scientific American*, 8 December 2009

A great example is when the prime minister of Australia said at an International
   Women's Day event ... Karp, Paul, 'Scott Morrison wants women to rise
   but not solely at expense of others', *The Guardian*, 8 March 2019

... in a time that Molloy refers to as 'when gay was a concept that had not
   been popularised'. Molloy, Shannon, *Fourteen: My year of darkness, and
   the light that followed*, Simon & Schuster (2020)

While stigma around LGBTQIA+ people is decreasing, one study recently showed that suicide rates ... Ream, Geoffrey L, 'What's unique about lesbian, gay, bisexual, and transgender (LGBT) youth and young adult suicides? Findings from the National Violent Death Reporting System', *Journal of Adolescent Health*, 2019, 64(5), 602–607

... Indigenous Australians, who make up just 3.3 per cent of Australia's population but 27 per cent of its prison population. Australian Law Reform Commission, 'Disproportionate incarceration rate', Australian Government, 9 January 2018

... the song 'Everyone's A Little Racist' from Avenue Q *may in fact be true.* Robert Lopez, Jeff Marx, John Tartaglia, Stephanie D'Abruzzo, Rick Lyon, 'Everyone's a Little Bit Racist', *Avenue Q (Original Broadway Cast Recording)*, BMG Music, 2003, track 5

Emmanuel Acho, author of Uncomfortable Conversations With a Black Man ... Acho, Emmanuel, *Uncomfortable Conversation with a Black Man*, Pan Macmillan UK (2020)

SECTION 5: ACTIVE CITIZENS

This is based on the work of Professor Ellen Langer from Harvard University ... No Stupid Questions, 'Are you as observant as you think?' Episode 50, 2 May 2021

Psychologist Dr Emily Lovegrove said that while teenagers have always sought knowledge and approval from their peers ... Beaty, Zoe, 'The kids are not alt-right: how extremist content infiltrates teen lives', *The Sydney Morning Herald*, 16 November 2019

Loretta Breuning, PhD, argues that 'Our brain is predisposed to go negative, and the news we consume reflects this' ... Heid, Markham, 'You asked; Is it bad for you to read the news constantly?', *Time*, 19 May 2020

There are great resources to talk about ethics ... Beard, Matt, Daniels, Molly, Smith, Carl (hosts), *Short & Curly*, ABC; Gaarder, Jostein, *Sophie's World*, Orion (2015); West, Philip, *Just Think: Philosophy puzzles for children aged 9 to 90*, Nielsen UK (2020)

... according to social psychologist and author Jonathan Haidt. Haidt, Jonathan, 'The moral roots of liberals and conservatives', TED, March 2008

Marcus Aurelius said that 'your mind will be like its habitual thoughts; for the soul becomes dyed by the colour of its thoughts'. Aurelius, Marcus, *Meditations*, Penguin Classics (2014)

Amanda Cox in The New York Times *wrote about how events that occur when you are 18* ... Cox, Amanda, 'How birth year influences political views', *The New York Times*, 7 July 2014

Open-mindedness, or the ability to switch to open-mindedness and what Daniel Kahneman would call 'slow thinking'... Kahneman, Daniel, *Thinking, Fast and Slow*, Penguin UK (2012)

SECTION 6: THE COACHING PARENT

One way to do this is what Dr Judith Locke would refer to as 'happy shrugging'. Locke, Judith, *The Bonsai Child*, Judith Locke (2015)

Dr Lisa Damour talks about teenagers, especially teenage girls, doing this and how it can be particularly upsetting for fathers. Damour, Lisa, *Ask Lisa: The psychology of parenting*, 'Dads & daughters, mothers & sons: How does gender shape parenting?', Episode 14, 10 November 2020

Take YouTube, for example. I cannot recommend the podcast 'Rabbit hole' more, it is so brilliant. Roose, Kevin, *Rabbit hole*, *The New York Times*

In her book How to Talk about Climate Change, *Dr Rebecca Huntley writes about the importance of teenage girls* ... Huntley, Rebecca, *How to Talk About Climate Change in a Way That Makes a Difference*, Murdoch Books (2020)

This relates to the psychological idea of 'lakes of comparison'. No Stupid Questions, 'How can you stop comparing yourself with other people?', Episode 13, 9 August 2020

The marshmallow test is a famous psychological test ... Mischel, Walter, *The Marshmallow Test: Understanding self-control and how to master it*, Random House UK (2015)

What you are dealing with here is my overactive imagination, and two very different loci of control. Joelson, Richard B, 'Locus of control: How do we determine our successes and failures?', *Psychology Today*, 2 August 2017

There are some great books that explore this. Stoppard, Tom, *Rosencrantz and Guildenstern Are Dead*, Faber & Faber (2005); Rhys, Jean, *Wide Sargasso Sea*, Penguin UK (2011); James, PD, *Death Comes to Pemberley*, Faber (2018); Miller, Madeleine, *Circe*, Bloomsbury (2019); Haynes, Natalie, *A Thousand Ships*, Pan Macmillan UK (2020)

Professor Martin Seligman, the founder of positive psychology ... Hall, Nicholas, 'Is feeling better as easy as ABC?', *Positive Psychology News*, 6 June 2007

When talking to ourselves, we fall into the trap of automatic negative thoughts (helpfully known as ANTs). Muris, Peter, Mayer, Birgit, den Adel, Madelon, Roos, Tamara and van Wamelen, Julie, 'Predictors of change following cognitive-behavioral treatment of children with anxiety problems: A preliminary investigation on negative automatic thoughts and anxiety control', *Child Psychiatry & Human Development*, 2009, 40(1), 139–151

There is a very neat visualisation by Lindsay Braman … Braman, Lindsay, lindsaybraman.com

People who regularly practise gratitude are healthier and happier. Sansone, Randy A and Sansone, Lori A, 'Gratitude and well being: The benefits of appreciation', *Psychiatry*, November 2010, 7(11), 18–22

Which rituals are important to you? Compan, E, Moreno, J, Ruiz, MT and Pascual, E, 'Doing things together: Adolescent health and family rituals', *Journal of Epidemiology & Community Health*, 2002, 56, 89–94

Evidence has shown that sharing meals can help a family develop their identity and model positive behavioural patterns. Compañ E, Moreno J, Ruiz MT, Pascual E, 'Doing things together: adolescent health and family rituals', *Journal of Epidemiology and Community Health*, 2002, 56(2), 89–94

There are many great books about grief I can point you to … Sales, Leigh, *Any Ordinary Day: Blindsides, resilience and what happens after the worst day of your life*, Penguin Australia (2019); Didion, Joan, *The Year of Magical Thinking*, HarperCollins Publishers (2006); Sandberg, Sheryl and Grant, Adam, *Option B: Facing adversity, building resilience, and finding joy*, Random House UK (2019)

Author Glennon Doyle writes that it took until she was a grown-up to realise … Excerpt from *Untamed* by Glennon Doyle, copyright © 2020 by Glennon Doyle. Used by permission of The Dial Press, an imprint of Random House, a division of Penguin Random House LLC. All rights reserved.

Even the process of Swedish death cleaning pre-empts grief … Magnusson, Margareta, *The Gentle Art of Swedish Death Cleaning: How to free yourself and your family from a lifetime of clutter*, Scribe (2017)

Glennon Doyle said a woman becomes a responsible adult … Excerpt from *Untamed* by Glennon Doyle, copyright © 2020 by Glennon Doyle. Used by permission of The Dial Press, an imprint of Random House, a division of Penguin Random House LLC. All rights reserved.

Acknowledgements

Where *50 Risks* was largely due to the people who shared my parenting journey, *50 Questions* has been thanks to the people who have shared my teenage years. Without lying about my age, I feel I have been a teenager thrice over: once as I aged between 12 and 18; again for the more than 10 years I have spent teaching teenagers; and finally now. In 2020 I separated from being a wife, and became a better mother, always a daughter, and surrounded by friends, seemingly in between it all. It is a very specific form of individuating.

In writing this book, I often cast my mind to the people who shared my teenage years, the people I loved so much, whom I have remained close to or reconnected with. Always first are Melissa Chan and Maria Wang-Faulkner. We became friends in Year 11, and through high school, university, long distances and short, they have been the two women I most admire. We have grown apart and back together, through shared experiences and stages, but are always, always there for each other. In anything I write about female friendship, it is of those two that my heart sings.

School is so important to a teenager, and we know that that feeling of belonging is the single biggest factor in a student's success. I belonged at Kincoppal Rose Bay as a teenager because it was a community that nurtured my quirks and taught me to write. I still carry its value of a social awareness that impels to action, and will occasionally break out into song, in French, when around anyone who attended.

Joseph Clayton and I have the cutest origin story, but it is too embarrassing to put in a book. We were at university together, and have been friends despite great distances (there's a theme here: my friends move overseas, why is that?). He came out to me over a Skype chat (those were the days) and he and his husband, Tyler, have a wonderful life that is too far away from me, a distance made greater by a pandemic. Our story is one I think of with love and laughter.

Shentel Lee and I became friends when I was in Year 12, connected by my then boyfriend and her best friend. I am forever grateful for our ongoing friendship, across the world, brought closer due to COVID.

My grandmother – Joanna, OG – my teenage years were more fun because of you. Yours was the suburb I was allowed to explore before any other, and it has been my home for over eight years.

Growing up with my brother, Alex, I was always safe. He was so protective of me that I found it embarrassing as a teen, but I now look at my own children and hope Jack will look after Alice like that. I look forward to sharing the teenage parenting years with you and Yvonne, and a lot of negronis.

My parents, Lucy and Malcolm, I think raised me to turn out exactly as I have, but I never knew it at the time. They believed in me and loved me when I was at my absolute least lovable. They talk about a certain parent–teacher night where they thought all hope was lost, but they knew I'd come good; if they hadn't, I don't think I would have. I love you both so much.

To Melissa, again, who has loved me as a teenager and through to my thirties.

To the people who I have educated teenagers with, and who remind me every day that relationships are at the heart of everything we do. The staff at St Catherine's – led by Julie Townsend, Kylie McCullah, Rebecca Herbert and Jo Graffen. I will always feel like a fraud in a room with you, because you are so brilliant

Elyse Read and René Mercer, the best bad humans a girl could ask for. Beatriz Cartlidge and Kylie Wilson, you are both so wonderful to work with. The year mentors who deal with teenagers every day and share a brilliant humour about it – Sarah Chapman, Caitlin Lamour, Sarah Charles, Karen Walton, Thea McLean, Sylvia Chronis, Bec and Jo.

I will make no secret of the past 18 months being strange but wonderful. I could not have laughed as much as I have without these people. Firstly, Daniel Meers and Bevan Shields – the three of us have been in constant conversation during lockdown and distance. They truly are the best of WhatsAppers.

Kumi has again been a friend, mentor, and sharer of memes and deep thoughts. I cannot mention memes without naming Sabina and her brother Ed, who have been great friends. Jason, who sends me psychology books as though I need them rather than just finding them interesting. I also thank him for Adelaide and Deb – thank you, ladies. Rebecca Huntley, my sister in single life and devoted motherhood. Jordan Baker, who brings a calm to everything. Charlie, who is an Insta friend who has helped me throughout the past year. Brenden and Shendi, your daughters Maddie and Lotte are a testament to your values. To Leigh, Jess and Mia, for frank and fun chats. To Julie, my editor at *The Sydney Morning Herald*, thank you for accepting my monthly rants.

To my neighbour Edwina, for coffees and margaritas and raising daughters and sons who respect each other, for dancing in the street and for excellent deliveries.

Michael, whose wholeness is in equal parts intimidating and inspiring, thank you for fixing many things.

To friends who have been supportive and caring from afar – Maureen and Todd, Joey Clayton, Bevan Shields. I wish the world would be the way it was but, as it is, it would be far worse without you.

Linda and Kaye, you are the greatest support and neighbours. I love you both very much. You are the greatest pair to make family out of friends. Sally, for constantly reminding me to be strong and for being in my corner.

The community at St Luke's, further apart with lockdown but always wise and nourishing. And, of course, I would be nowhere without the team and faces at Wolf Cafe. And to Danica and the team at Lagree who kept me sane. I write this in lockdown missing you terribly.

To the people who made this book: thank you, Arwen, for believing in a book idea on WhatsApp. We have used *50 Risks* for our own parenting journeys, and I know this will sit on our shelves until we need it when our kids are teenagers. Thank you for your support and unwavering belief. To Loran, Vanessa and Sinéad – again, I still haven't met you, but you all rock. To Sandy Grant and Fiona Hardie, for letting a kid you used to know write books. Thank you. They have already been thanked in one of the questions, but a special thanks to Maria Wang-Faulkner, Jordan Shea and Shannon Molloy. You are wonderful.

Thank you to the friends who read this before it was ready – Kumi, Grace, Rebecca, Melissa, Kathleen, Ian, Jess and Zac.

To my children, Jack and Alice, who are not yet teenagers. I see moments of your teenage personality come through and I shiver with excitement and fear. I hope that this book helps us navigate what will be testing times, and that you grow to be independent, resilient, compassionate, and taller than me. Get ready for question time.

Thank you all for reading this.
I hope it starts great conversations.

Published in 2022 by Hardie Grant Books, an imprint of Hardie Grant Publishing

Hardie Grant Books (Melbourne)
Wurundjeri Country
Building 1, 658 Church Street
Richmond, Victoria 3121

Hardie Grant Books (London)
5th & 6th Floors
52–54 Southwark Street
London SE1 1UN

hardiegrantbooks.com

A catalogue record for this book is available from the National Library of Australia

50 Questions to Ask Your Teens
ISBN 978 1 74379 782 2

10 9 8 7 6 5 4 3 2 1

Publisher: Arwen Summers
Project Editor: Loran McDougall
Editor: Vanessa Lanaway
Design Manager: Kristin Thomas
Designer and illustrator: Sinéad Murphy
Production Manager: Todd Rechner

Colour reproduction by Splitting Image Colour Studio
Printed in China by Leo Paper Products LTD.

The paper this book is printed on is from FSC®-certified forests and other sources. FSC® promotes environmentally responsible, socially beneficial and economically viable management of the world's forests.

Hardie Grant acknowledges the Traditional Owners of the country on which we work, the Wurundjeri people of the Kulin nation and the Gadigal people of the Eora nation, and recognises their continuing connection to the land, waters and culture. We pay our respects to their Elders past, present and emerging.